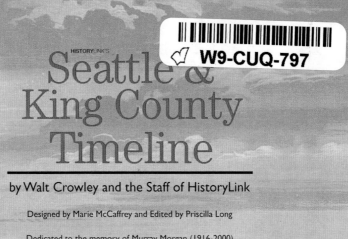

HISTORYLINK'S
Seattle & King County Timeline

by Walt Crowley and the Staff of HistoryLink

Designed by Marie McCaffrey and Edited by Priscilla Long

Dedicated to the memory of Murray Morgan (1916-2000)
Historian, Author, Teacher

W9-CUQ-797

A HistoryLink Book

Published by History Ink in association with the University of Washington Press

With special support from Jon and Bobbe Bridge, the Hugh & Jane Ferguson Foundation, Greater Seattle Chamber of Commerce, the Joshua Green Foundation, King County Landmarks & Heritage Commission, Litho Craft, John McClelland Jr., Microsoft Corporation, Seattle Public Utilities, Chris Smith Towne, and the Washington Mutual Foundation

Copyright 2001, History Ink. All Rights Reserved.

History Ink & HistoryLink, 1425 Fourth Avenue, Suite 710, Seattle, WA; Tel: 206-447-8140; Web: www.historylink.org; Email: Admin@historylink.org

First printing: November 13, 2001, at Litho Craft, Inc., Lynnwood
Second printing: July 2002

ISBN 0-295-98165-2

Illustrations courtesy of the Museum of History & Industry, University of Washington Libraries Special Collections, Library of Congress, Paul Dorpat, David Eskenazi, Art Hupy, Alan Lande, Anthony Powell, Mary Randlett, John Stamets, The Seattle Times, Seattle Post-Intelligencer, Seattle Mariners, Vulcan Northwest, Woodland Park Zoo Society, and Boeing Archives.

This book is based on content prepared by HistoryLink staff and contributing writers in cooperation with leading historical societies, scholars, and educational institutions. HistoryLink is a registered U.S. trademark of History Ink, a 501(c)(3) tax-exempt non-profit corporation.

Walt Crowley, President and Executive Director

Priscilla Long, Senior Editor

Marie McCaffrey, Art Director

Chris Goodman, Site Administrator

Paul Dorpat, Senior Historian

Greg Lange, Alan Stein, Cassandra Tate, Ph.D., and David W. Wilma, Staff Historians

Patrick McRoberts and Alyssa Burrows, Associate Editors

Steven Leith, Technologist

HistoryLink

Introduction

HistoryLink

About us

Search

Help

Galleries

People's History

Visitor center

Contact us

Links plus

Pan

Sponsors

This little book traces the evolution of Seattle and King County, Washington, from the arrival of the first permanent white settlers in the fall of 1851 through to the fall of 2001. It is intended to offer a quick and, we hope, entertaining introduction to our community's history over the past 150 years.

Seattle was forged in the industrial revolution by self-aware city builders, and its subsequent development reflects the commercial, technological, and social dynamics of American capitalism and democracy with unique clarity. That metropolitan King County took form in a mere 150 years — the span of just two average human lifetimes — makes this story all the more remarkable, exciting, and accessible.

Of course, it is impossible to compress 150 years of human enterprise and struggle into 100 pages — or even 10,000 pages — which is why we created HistoryLink (www.historylink.org), the nation's first online encyclopedia of community history written expressly for the Internet.

HistoryLink offers free access to a growing database of thousands of original, authoritative, and easily searchable essays and features detailing all of the subjects, events, and persons described in the pages to follow — and much, much more. We hope that this book will serve as your portal to our region's rich past and inspire you to explore on your own via www.historylink.org, books, museums, archives, libraries, and other repositories of local lore and history.

12,000 BCE ~ 1850:
When Worlds Collide

The relentless collision of the great Pacific and North American tectonic plates raised western Washington from the sea and extruded the Cascades over tens of millions of years. Then, about 14,000 years ago, nature set the stage for the human drama to follow. As the last great Ice Age ended, the retreating Vashon Glacier gouged out the Puget Sound basin, leaving behind most of today's major lakes, hills, ridges, and river valleys. Volcanic eruptions, earthquakes, floods, landslides, and gradual erosion continue to rearrange the scenery to the present day.

Sir Francis Drake

Scientists estimate that human beings entered the scene about 2,000 years later from Asia. They crossed the land bridge that once linked Siberia and Alaska, and migrated south along the Pacific Coast.

Most early residents of the Puget Sound basin spoke one or another dialect of the Puget Sound Salish language, known to its speakers as Lushootseed or Whulshootseed. Other related languages in the Salish family were spoken over a large part of the Northwest Coast and in some areas east of the Cascade Mountains.

Major groups or tribes of local native peoples included the Suquamish, Duwamish, Nisqually, Snoqualmie, and today's

Muckleshoots (actually several distinct tribes). The original citizens of what is now Western Washington established a way of life closely fitted to the resources and cycles of the region's coasts, rivers, lakes, and forests. Except for occasional local clashes and raids by northern tribes, Puget Sound's first peoples led a peaceful and culturally rich existence — unaware of another group of tribes that was venturing westward from a distant continent.

George Vancouver

Old World Meets the New

By the late 1500s, Europeans had "discovered" the Pacific Ocean and were exploring the western coastline of North America. They sought riches such as gold and furs, strategic advantages over rival nations, and, above all, a fabled Northwest Passage that would provide a shortcut between the North Atlantic and Pacific. The Spanish came first, soon followed by the British pirate-explorer Sir Francis Drake and then the Russian explorer Vitus Bering. The urgency of exploration was sharpened by the claim of a Greek sailor, known as Juan de Fuca, that the Pacific mouth of the Northwest Passage lay somewhere between 47 and 48 degrees latitude.

British Captain Charles Barkley discovered de Fuca's strait in 1787 while seeking sea otter pelts. Spanish explorer Manuel Quimper charted the channel three years later and penetrated as far as the San Juan Islands. Had Spain pushed a little farther south, this book might be written *en Espanol*; instead, the honor of being the first

In May 1792, British explorer George Vancouver surveys Puget Sound while U.S. explorer Robert Gray enters the Columbia River.

Lewis and Clark arrive at the mouth of the Columbia in October 1805.

Great Britain and the United States agree to joint occupation of Oregon (including present-day Washington and Idaho) on October 20, 1818.

Hudson's Bay Company (HBC) establishes Fort Nisqually on southern Puget Sound in April 1833.

HBC launches Puget Sound's first steamship, *Beaver*, in November 1836.

U.S. Captain Charles Wilkes begins survey of Puget Sound on May 11, 1841, and later names Elliott Bay.

U.S. settlers in Oregon create "provisional government" on May 2, 1843.

Great Britain signs "Treaty of Oregon," ceding its Northwest claims below the 49th parallel on June 15, 1846.

ABOARD THE *BEAVER*:

On about November 12, 1836, the Hudson's Bay Company ship *Beaver,* the first steamship to travel on Puget Sound, passed by King County. The ship carried two 35 horsepower wood-fueled steam engines, and consumed 40 cords of wood to travel an average of 30 miles per day. The *Beaver* worked Puget Sound and nearby waters until running aground at the entrance to the Vancouver, B.C., harbor in 1888.

U.S. establishes Territory of Oregon on August 14, 1848, while California gold rush spurs western migration.

Donation Land Act grants each Oregon settler 320 acres of "free" land effective September 27, 1850.

PUGET'S SOUND

On May 19, 1792, the British sloop-of-war *Discovery* dropped anchor between Bainbridge and Blake islands. The following morning, Capt. George Vancouver dispatched Lt. Peter Puget and Master Joseph Whidbey to conduct a detailed survey of the waters to the south. The Vancouver expedition charted and named numerous landmarks, including Mt. Rainier (for British Admiral Peter Rainier), Whidbey Island, and Hood Canal, and the waters south of Bainbridge Island became known as "Puget's Sound." Contacts with the natives were cordial if mutually wary, and legend maintains that a very young Chief Seattle witnessed Vancouver's arrival on Puget Sound.

Europeans to enter Puget Sound fell to George Vancouver and his British Navy crew.

It is possible that a young boy and future chief we know today as Seattle watched Vancouver's ship *Discovery* drop anchor off Bainbridge Island on May 19, 1792. Vancouver dispatched Lt. Peter Puget to "sound" the waters that now bear his name, and dubbed a towering, snowcapped volcano "Rainier" for his patron admiral. Vancouver also noted that many natives bore the scars of earlier smallpox — one of several virulent diseases which accompanied European explorers and traders to the Pacific Northwest. This alien invasion would ultimately kill tens of thousands of the region's original inhabitants, who lacked natural immunity to Old World microbes.

Union Jack or Old Glory?

Britain soon replaced Spain as temporary sovereign of the Pacific Northwest. The United States staked its own claims thanks to Captain Robert Gray's entry into the Columbia River at virtually the same moment Vancouver was exploring Puget Sound. The overland expedition to the Pacific led by Meriwether Lewis and William Clark in 1804-1805 provided more detail on the Pacific Northwest, and American ships and British traders of the Hudson's Bay Company soon followed to exploit the region's rich bounty of sea otters and other fur-bearing animals. There seemed to be enough for all, so Britain and the U.S. agreed in 1818 to "joint

occupation" of what was by then called Oregon (a name with murky origins).

The Hudson's Bay Company established the first permanent European settlement on Puget Sound near the mouth of the Nisqually River in 1833. U.S. Captain Charles Wilkes arrived in 1841 and started a naval survey of the Sound at "Commencement Bay." He also named a smaller bay for one (or all) of three crew members with the last name Elliott.

Within a few years, U.S. citizens outnumbered British subjects in Oregon. These Yankees established their own provisional government in 1843 and sought U.S. recognition. To avoid war, Britain gave up its claims to Oregon below the 49th parallel in 1846, and Oregon became a U.S. territory two years later. Settlement accelerated with passage of the Donation Land Act of 1850, which granted Oregon settlers up to 320 acres of free land (notwithstanding the rights of the native residents). Thousands were soon pouring west along the Oregon Trail to the Willamette Valley.

A venturesome few pushed north across the Columbia River to lay claims on Puget Sound — and thereby raised the curtain on the next act in our history.

RULE BRITANNIA

The Hudson's Bay Company (HBC) established a stockade and trading post in April near Sequalitchew Creek on the Nisqually Delta, which became the first permanent European settlement on Puget Sound. The HBC's Puget's Sound Agricultural Company later founded "Cowlitz Farm" near the fort in 1838 and tolerated the growing number of United States citizens who raised cattle and crops in the vicinity. HBC also welcomed Catholic missionaries such as Bishop Modeste Demers, who conducted the first Christian religious services at the fort in April 1838 and in Seattle in 1852, and baptized Chief "Noah" Seattle among other many other natives. Pictured above: A.M.A. Blanchet, F.N. Blanchet, and M. Demers

A WHALE OF A MISSION

On May 11, 1841, the U.S. Navy ships *Vincennes* and *Porpoise*, commanded by Capt. Charles Wilkes, dropped anchor in southern Puget Sound and their crews proceeded to chart Puget Sound and name numerous landmarks, including Commencement Bay and Elliott Bay. This United States Exploring Expedition marked America's first formal entry into Puget Sound waters. Wilkes was an ambitious and autocratic officer who took command of the United States Exploring Expedition in 1838 with the aim of circumnavigating the globe and charting Antarctica and the Pacific Coast of North America. By the time he returned to Norfolk, Virginia, in 1842, his fleet of six ships had dwindled to two. Word of Wilkes' harsh discipline and personal arrogance earned him public rebuke and inspired Herman Melville's most famous character, Captain Ahab. The expedition report helped to establish Oregon and Puget Sound as new prizes for America's manifest destiny.

1851~1860: New York Alki

Many different reasons and ambitions motivated the swelling numbers of settlers who trudged 2,000 miles westward from St. Louis along the Oregon Trail. Some sought quick riches from gold or silver, some were lured by the federal promise of free land, some merely wanted to escape the confines of established society (and not a few, slavery), and a few dreamed of building whole new cities in the "wilderness."

Among the last, the Denny and Boren families — later joined by the Bells and Lows — sold their Illinois farms and loaded all they could carry into four wagons to head west on April 10, 1851. Their goal was the fertile Willamette Valley but they would end up hundreds of miles north on Puget Sound.

By then, news of Puget Sound's natural beauty and potential bounty was already attracting settlers north from Oregon City to Fort Nisqually and the new village of Olympia. The Sound had also been cited in 1846 as the ideal terminus for a transcontinental railroad intended to link Pacific trade with the Great Lakes.

A young Iowan named John Holgate and his native guides canoed down the Sound in the summer of 1850. He realized that the valley of the meandering Duwamish River offered ideal farmland, but departed without staking a claim. Meanwhile Luther Collins, Henry Van Asselt, and Jacob and Samuel Maple (sometimes spelled Mapel), also scouted Puget Sound and admired the same Duwamish bottomland that had impressed Holgate. They arrived on September 14, 1851, and staked claims two days later.

On the Beach

Within a week the Duwamish pioneers were visited by a young David Denny and John Low, sent north from Oregon City to scout the Sound. The two were joined in Olympia by Lee Terry who, with his brother Charles, had recently arrived from New York. Both Lee Terry and

Inset: the schooner Exact

Right: Chief Seattle closed his eyes for his only known photograph.

MAP
OF THE
OREGON TERRITORY
BY THE
U. S. Ex. Ex.
CHARLES WILKES Esqr.
COMMANDER.
1841.

John Low staked claims near today's Alki Point. Low hired his companions to build a cabin before returning south with a note from David Denny urging his older brother Arthur to "come as soon as you can."

And so he did. On the drizzly morning of November 13, 1851, the schooner *Exact* dropped anchor off Alki beach. Once assembled on the strand, the "Denny Party" numbered just two dozen men, women, and children. Confronted with the sight of the unfinished, roofless cabin, William Bell said the women "sat on a log and took a big cry."

The arrival of these new neighbors was carefully monitored by the area's Duwamish and Suquamish residents, and especially by their chief, Seattle, who personally welcomed the settlers. He calculated that the whites would bring trading goods and offer protection from raids by northern tribes. Some 1,000 of his people soon camped around Alki and fed the settlers during the winter of 1851-1852. Chief Seattle also encouraged Olympia physician and merchant David "Doc" Maynard to join the settlement the following spring.

Picking Up Stakes

Of the Alki group, Charles Terry was the most bullish. He dubbed the nascent village "New York," to which skeptics added the tag "Alki," meaning "by and by" in the Chinook trading jargon. Arthur Denny, William Bell, and Carson Boren did not share Terry's optimism. After surveying nearby waters, they laid claims to the steep ridges cradling Elliott Bay on February 15, 1852, while Maynard took possession of the low peninsula and nearby mudflats where Pioneer Square, the International District, and Seattle's sports stadiums now stand.

The village first called itself "Duwamps," but Maynard had a better suggestion: Seattle (which is closer to the true Lushootseed pronunciation than "Sealth," although such appropriation of one's name was frowned on in Salish culture). The community's

Timeline

Luther Collins, Henry Van Asselt, and Jacob and Samuel Maple select first Donation Land claims in King County on September 16, 1851.

John Low and Lee Terry select claims at Alki Point on September 28, 1851.

Denny party lands at Alki Point on November 13, 1851.

Charles Terry opens "New York Store," first in future King County, by November 28, 1851.

Settlers begin loading logs on the ship *Leonesa* in King County's first export on December 9, 1851.

Arthur Denny, Carson Boren, and William Bell select first claims on Elliott Bay on February 15, 1852.

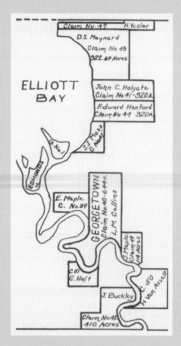

ELLIOTT BAY

Claim No. 47   H. Yesler
D.S. Maynard
Claim No. 43
322.64 Acres
John C. Holgate
Claim No. 41 - 320 A.
Edward Hanford
Claim No. 44 320 A.
J.J. Moss
G. Maple
GEORGETOWN
E. Maple
C. No. 39
L.M. Collins
Claim No. 0-644
S. Maple
Claim No. 40-644
148 Acres
C. 81
G. Holt
J. Buckley
C. 40
H. Van Asselt
Claim No. 42
410 Acres
S. No. 1
EDMONDS

WHO'S ON FIRST?

During the late summer of 1850, young John Cornelius Holgate explored the Duwamish River and considered claiming a site in future Georgetown. After a brief sojourn, Holgate headed south and did not return to Puget Sound until 1853, when he staked a claim on Beacon Hill.

The honor of being King County's first white settlers belongs to Luther Collins, Henry Van Asselt, and Jacob and Samuel Maple (or Mapel), who arrived near the mouth of the Duwamish on September 14, 1851 — not in June, as one descendent later claimed — and later collected their families.

The Denny Party is rightly credited as being Seattle's first settlers based less on their November 13, 1851, arrival than on their relocation to Elliott Bay the following spring. Unlike their neighbors, this group and other early settlers such as Doc Maynard articulated and advanced a vision of a future city where Seattle stands today.

Louisa and David Denny with their first children

THE ROSTER OF KING COUNTY AND SEATTLE'S FIRST PERMANENT WHITE SETTLERS

THE COLLINS PARTY

Luther Collins, about 37
Diana Borst Collins, about 36
Lucinda Collins, 13 or 14
Stephen Collins, about 7
Jacob Maple, 53
Samuel A. Maple, 23
Henry Van Asselt, 34

THE DENNY PARTY

Arthur Armstrong Denny, 29
Mary Ann (Boren) Denny, 28
David T. Denny, 19
Louisa Catherine "Kate" Denny, 7
Margaret Lenora Denny, 4
Rolland H. Denny, 6 weeks
John N. Low, 31
Lydia Low, 31
Mary L. Low, 8
Alonzo Low, 6
John V. Low, 4
Minerva Low, 2

Carson D. Boren, 26
Mary Boren, 20
Livonia Gertrude Boren, 11 months
Louisa Boren, 24
William N. Bell, 34
Sarah Ann Bell, 32
Laura Keziah Bell, 8
Olive Julia Bell, 5
Mary Virginia Bell, 4
Alvina Lavina Bell, 9 months
Charles C. Terry, 22
Leander (Lee) Terry, 33

King County Founders: Arthur Denny, Louisa and Mary Ann Boren, Henry Van Asselt, Jacob Maple, John and Lydia Low

fortunes were boosted tremendously in October 1852 when Henry Yesler chose it as the site for Puget Sound's first steam-powered sawmill. Two months later, the Oregon Territorial Legislature named Seattle as the seat of a new King County.

Charles Terry

Arthur Denny also campaigned to have the town designated as the capital of Washington Territory when it was created in March 1853, but that honor went to Olympia. The founding territorial legislature also missed the opportunity to become the first U.S. jurisdiction to enfranchise women by rejecting a suffrage amendment by a single vote.

The new Territory differed from Oregon on one significant point: Washington did not ban the residency of African Americans, and it soon attracted numerous black settlers. One of the first was Manuel Lopes, a barber who is credited with establishing one of Seattle's first businesses.

Catholic Bishop Modeste Demers holds Seattle's first Christian ceremony on August 22, 1852.

Henry Yesler arrives in October 1852 and starts buliding Puget Sound's first steam-powered sawmill.

King County is created by Oregon Territorial Legislature on December 22, 1852, and Seattle is named its County Seat.

Doc Maynard issues King County's first marriage license and officiates as David Denny and Louisa Boren wed on January 23, 1853.

President Fillmore signs law creating Washington Territory on March 2, 1853.

Growing Pains

Henry Yesler built his sawmill on a wharf at the foot of today's Yesler Way. It was called Mill Street then, and contrary to many accounts, there is little evidence that the steep muddy path was used as a "Skid Road" for logs. With Seattle's future seemingly secure, its founding settlers sat down in May 1853 to lay out the street plans (called "plats") for the metropolis to come.

They couldn't agree on whether roads should follow the topography or the compass, which is why north-south streets remain tangled along today's Yesler Way.

Sharper conflicts lay ahead. Settlers were beginning to fill the village and nearby forests, and the original residents chafed at the loss of traditional trails, camps, and hunting grounds,

A MAN, A PLAN, A CANAL...

Most of Seattle's few hundred residents gathered near a lake called "tenas Chuck" ("little waters") to celebrate the Fourth of July in 1854. In a speech to the group, Thomas Mercer advocated naming the larger lake to the east, known variously as hyas Chuck, Geneva, and D'wamish, as Lake Washington. He also called for renaming tenas Chuck as Lake Union because he believed that a canal would ultimately connect it to Lake Washington and Puget Sound. The Lake Washington Ship canal was finally completed in 1934 — a mere 80 years after Mercer first proposed it.

Sketch of Yesler's Mill

First plats filed for "Town of Seattle" on May 23, 1853.

Woman suffrage amendment to Washington Territory constitution fails by one vote on February 28, 1854.

Native workers in front of Yesler's Cookhouse

not to mention the increasingly arrogant demeanor of their former "guests." Tensions did not ease when Washington Territory's first governor, Colonel Isaac Stevens, arrived in late 1853 with one overriding mission: negotiate treaties that would remove Indian tribes from most of their ancestral lands. Chief Seattle greeted Stevens on his first visit to Seattle in January 1854, and warned him, "Be just and deal kindly with my people, for the dead are not altogether powerless."

Nor were the living. After the conclusion of several major treaties in 1854 and 1855, some natives raided farms in the Duwamish and Green River valleys, and whites retaliated with lynchings and deadly assaults on villages. Chief Leschi led a daylong attack on Seattle itself on January 26, 1856, but was repelled by U.S. Navy marines and artillery. The federal government later captured and hanged Leschi on unrelated (and false) murder charges.

Henry Yesler

The "Battle of Seattle" shook the confidence of some like Doc Maynard, who swapped Pioneer Square for Charles Terry's Alki claim in perhaps the dumbest real estate transaction in local history. But the town survived and resumed steady if slow growth. Yesler's mill loaded lumber on ships bound for San Francisco and Hawaii, and the salmon saltery and other maritime suppliers did a brisk trade. Coal was discovered south and east of the village and would soon become another valuable export.

Downtown Seattle in 1859

Other signs of civilization also showed themselves as the "better element" attended Methodist Episcopal services in the White

Nisqually Chief Leschi

Church, named for its paint and founded by minister David Blaine, while his wife Catharine taught in the town's first school. Others flocked to a growing number of saloons and brothels such as Capt. Felker's house, which was run by a huge, tart-tongued Irishwoman christened Mary Conklin but known to most as "Madame Damnable."

The census of 1860 enumerated 302 non-Indians living in King County, two-thirds of whom resided in Seattle proper. The community ranked only 12th out of the Territory's 19 counties, but Seattle's leaders had just started building their city "by and by."

"A CLAP OF THUNDER FROM A CLEAR SKY"

Chief Seattle, or si?al in his native Lushootseed language, was born in the 1780s. He led the Duwamish and Suquamish tribes as the first Euro-American settlers arrived in the 1850s. Baptized Noah by Modeste Demers, Seattle was regarded as a "firm friend of the Whites," and a respected leader among Salish tribes. He is also credited with a famous speech welcoming Territorial Governor Isaac Stevens to Seattle in January 1854. The only account of this prophetic and melancholy oration was published 33 years later by pioneer Dr. Henry Smith, who likened Seattle's voice to "a clap of thunder from a clear sky." Seattle signed the Point Elliott (Mukilteo) Treaty of 1855, which relinquished tribal claims to most of the area, and retired to the Suquamish Reservation at Port Madison, where he died on June 7, 1866.

Territorial Seal and Governor Isaac Stevens

Settlers retreat to blockhouse during Battle of Seattle

Native American tribes sign treaties at Medicine Creek on December 26, 1854, and Point Elliott (Mukilteo) on January 22, 1855, accepting relocation to Puget Sound reservations.

Seattle's first church (Methodist Episcopal) is dedicated on May 12, 1855.

Native Americans attack settlers along White River between Kent and Auburn on October 28, 1855.

Native Americans attack Seattle on January 26, 1856.

U. S. troops kill Nisqually women and children during Indian wars in April 1856.

Nisqually Chief Leschi is hanged on February 19, 1858.

Military Road is completed in 1860 between Fort Vancouver on the Columbia River and Seattle.

HENRY YESLER'S "WIVES"

On June 12, 1855, the daughter of Duwamish Chief Curly bore a child. Although the infant appears in the record as Julia Benson, it was widely accepted that she was actually sired by pioneer industrialist Henry Yesler. Julia grew up to marry Port Townsend treasurer Charles Intermela, and upon her death in 1907, newspaper obituaries listed Yesler as her father.

Yesler had arrived in Seattle in October 1852 and chose the crude village as the site of his sawmill. During its construction and early operations, he employed Chief Curly and formed a de facto marriage with the chief's daughter (whose name has vanished from the record). Yesler's wife Sarah remained in Ohio until traveling west in 1858, at which time Julia was taken in by Jeremiah Benson. She later joined the Yesler household as a servant before moving to California for the rest of her youth.

Such liaisons and formal marriages between white men and Indian women were routine in early Seattle. Historian Edmund Meany speculated that if a failed proposal for woman suffrage had included Indian as well as white females in 1854, Washington Territory might have become the first U.S. jurisdiction to enfranchise women.

The Man Who Invented Seattle...

Or so historian-journalist Bill Speidel dubbed David S. "Doc" Maynard. On the advice of Chief Seattle, the Vermont-born physician relocated from Olympia to the tiny village of Duwamps (Seattle's original name) in the spring of 1852 and served as its first physician, merchant, Indian agent, and justice of the peace. Maynard founded the town's first general store, the Seattle Exchange, and urged his neighbors to rename the town to honor Chief Seattle.

In May 1853, Arthur Denny sat down with Doc Maynard to lay out streets on their claims and that of Carson Boren. As Denny later told the story, Maynard came to the table "stimulated by liquor" and decided "that he was not only monarch of all he surveyed but what Boren and I surveyed as well." Maynard stubbornly insisted on orienting his streets according to the cardinal points of the compass (his holdings being mostly flat, when not submerged by the tide) while Denny and Boren laid theirs out to parallel the shore and steep ridges of their claims on Elliott Bay. Denny and Maynard could not reach agreement and filed conflicting plats on May 23. The legacy survives in the tangle of mismatched roads along Yesler Way (then called Mill Street or "Skid Road") where the pioneers' divergent street grids abut. We might add that the political dichotomy symbolized by Denny's sober conservatism and Maynard's liberal humanism also seems to have endured.

Lt. S. Phelps' sketch and map of 1856 Seattle, with later plats superimposed

1861~1880: Settling In

Rev. Daniel Bagley

After the hardship and turmoil of its first decade, Seattle now took time to put its house in order. It was relatively unruffled by Abraham Lincoln's election and the ensuing Civil War, news of which took up to three weeks to reach Seattle by steamer or horseback.

Arthur Denny tried again to woo the state capital from Olympia, but settled for the Territorial University instead on the advice of Methodist Protestant pastor Daniel Bagley, who established Seattle's second ("Brown") church in 1860. Asa Shinn Mercer was hired as the University's teacher and president, and convened its first classes, which included all ages and grades, on November 4, 1861.

The University occupied a handsome two-story building atop "Denny's Knoll" on the site of today's Four Seasons Olympic Hotel (the original columns survive on the present UW campus). It was built chiefly by John Pike, who also dug the first shallow log canal breaching Montlake between Lake Washington and Union in 1861, and is the eponym of downtown Seattle's Pike Street.

Timeline

John Pike digs shallow Montlake log canal to connect Union Bay and Portage Bay in 1861.

African American pioneer William Grose arrives in Seattle in 1861.

Territorial University (University of Washington) opens on November 4, 1861.

Coal is discovered at Newcastle in October 1863.

Seattle's first newspaper, the *Seattle Gazette*, is published on December 10, 1863.

African American property owner William Hedges arrives in Seattle in 1864.

Mercer Girls reach Seattle on May 16, 1864.

First telegraph line to Seattle is completed on October 25, 1864.

Tourists visit Snoqualmie Falls for the first time in 1865.

Territorial University on Denny's Knoll

Red, Black, and Suburban

Following a bitterly cold winter, smallpox reappeared in King County in the spring of 1862. The plague was spread along the Northwest coast by a single steamer, and claimed the lives of as many as 14,000 North Coast Indians — many of whom could have been saved if white officials and physicians had intervened with prompt quarantines and vaccinations.

The city had welcomed its second African American resident in 1861. William Grose would become a prominent restaurateur and establish the city's first black community in Madison Valley. He was joined a few years later by William Hedges, a fugitive slave who later helped to develop Green Lake and other "suburban" neighborhoods, and by another African American chef, Matthias Monet.

The town's black population numbered 13 by the decade's end. The census neglected to count the first 30 or so Chinese immigrant workers whose numbers would quickly swell and play an essential role in Seattle's early development.

As the area's population diversified it also spread outward. Establishment of rural post offices with names such as Squak (ultimately Issaquah) and Slaughter (named for an Army officer killed in the Indian Wars of 1855-56, now Auburn) represented the future seeds of suburban King County, which ranked fourth in the Territory by 1870 with more than 2,100 settlers.

William Grose

News and Blues

In December 1863, Seattle's first newspaper, the *Gazette*, began publication. The only thing Seattle's mostly male population craved more than news was female companionship. Brothel operators such as John Pinnell were happy to meet the need with a mostly native staff, but

Early tourist at Snoqualmie Falls

City of Seattle incorporates for the first time on January 14, 1865, but is later dissolved due to citizen complaints.

Chief Seattle dies on June 7, 1866.

Weekly Intelligencer newspaper founded in Seattle in 1867.

On January 27, 1867, new post offices open to serve settlers of White River (later Kent), Slaughter (Auburn), and Black River (Renton).

Seattle Library Association is organized on August 7, 1868.

Seattle's first Catholic Church is built in 1869.

Seattle city government is re-incorporated by Territorial Legislature on December 2, 1869, and Henry Atkins is named its first mayor.

Dexter Horton establishes King County's first bank in March 1870.

On May 20, 1870, new post offices open to serve Snoqualmie (now North Bend) and Squak (now Issaquah).

On May 16, 1864, Asa Shinn Mercer returned to Seattle with 11 "Mercer Girls" chiefly recruited from Lowell, Massachusetts. Mercer brought a second group of "Mercer Girls" or "Mercer's Belles" on May 28, 1866. The young women were to work as teachers and served to increase the number of marriageable women in a Territory populated chiefly by young bachelors. All but one wed and most made important contributions to elevating the level of Seattle's frontier culture and society. A century later, the Mercer Girls' tale inspired the TV series "Here Come the Brides." Perry Como sang the show's tongue-in-cheek theme lyric," ...The bluest skies you've ever seen are in Seattle."

Harpers Weekly etching of Mercer's Belles. Right: Asa Mercer, Catherine Stevens, Georgia Pearson, Sara Jane Gallagher, and Elizabeth Ordway

Seattle's first public schoolhouse opens on August 15, 1870.

Arrival of Northern Pacific Railroad surveyors in August 1870 triggers sudden "Queen City" real estate boom and first East Coast investments.

Susan B. Anthony helps found Washington Woman Suffrage Association on October 1, 1871.

Western Washington's first railroad transports coal from Lake Union to Pike Street on March 25, 1872.

some men sought more "genteel" company. Town leaders agreed and dispatched Asa Mercer to New England to recruit single women suitable for marriage, teaching, and other civilizing pursuits. He returned on May 16, 1864, with 11 women who had braved the long ocean voyage via pre-canal Panama. A second wave of 34 more "Mercer Girls" arrived in 1866.

The first Western Union telegraph line entered service on October 25, 1864. The following April it flashed the happy news of Robert E. Lee's surrender — followed days later by the bulletin of Abraham Lincoln's assassination. The entire town gathered at the Territorial University to mourn their martyred president.

Chief Seattle's death on June 7, 1866, at the Suquamish Tribe's Port Madison reservation elicited far less response, at least initially. That same year Seattle leaders — including pioneers personally aided by the Chief — petitioned the federal government against granting the Duwamish tribe its own reservation. Perhaps motivated by a tinge of guilt, a delegation of Seattle dignitaries installed a marble headstone on the Chief's grave in 1890. Meanwhile, the Duwamish were scattered among several regional reservations but continue to campaign for a home of their own.

Housekeeping

The young city spent much of the second half of the 1860s establishing essential institutions. Seattle's first try at self-government in 1865 ended in a taxpayers' revolt and repeal of its original incorporation. The Territorial Legislature imposed a new city charter in 1869 and appointed Henry Atkins as Seattle's first mayor.

Fr. Prefontaine and his Church

17

The new Seattle Library Association had better luck under the guidance of Sarah Yesler, and began lending books in 1869 (this task was assumed by city government in 1890). That same year, her husband Henry built Yesler Hall, which served as the town's main social and entertainment center. In 1870, Mercer recruit Elizabeth "Lizzie" Ordway rang the bell to summon students to Seattle's first public school.

The Catholic Church returned to Seattle in 1867 after a long absence. Although Nisqually Bishop Modeste Demers had conducted Seattle's first Christian service back in 1852 and purchased a church site in 1858, the Diocese wrote off the town as a white Protestant stronghold. Father Francis Xavier Prefontaine disagreed strenuously and fought for permission to build a church, Our Lady of Good Help, which he opened in 1869.

Ice is sold in Seattle for the first time on May 13, 1872, and the first ice cream is made available five days later.

Seattle's first amateur baseball club, the Dolly Varden, forms in July 1872.

Schwabacher's erects Seattle's first brick building on October 24, 1872.

Seattle Mayor C. P. Stone embezzles $15,000 and flees town on February 23, 1873.

Harbingers

The United States' purchase of Alaska from Russia in 1867 created a new market for Seattle-based businesses and media. The town's second newspaper, the *Weekly Intelligencer*, hit the streets in 1867, followed by *The Alaska Times* in 1870.

The San Francisco dry goods merchants, Schwabacher & Sons, opened a Seattle store in 1869 and dispatched Bailey Gatzert to manage it. He built the town's first true brick building the following year, earned respect in the community, and became Seattle's first Jewish mayor in 1875. Meanwhile in 1870, Dexter Horton established the town's first bank in a safe in the backroom of his general store. It later grew to become SeaFirst Bank before merging with Bank of America.

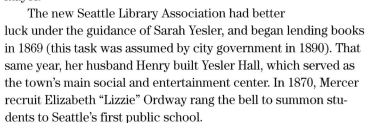

Sarah Yesler and her mansion at 3rd and James, which housed the Seattle Public Library until it burned on January 1, 1901

1861~1880

Early home of the Weekly Intelligencer

With some 1,150 residents, Seattle was the Territory's third largest city by 1870. It was ready for its next step forward just as Northern Pacific Railroad surveyors arrived on a quest to identify the best terminus for the nation's next great transcontinental railway. Seattle and the rest of the region would soon develop a one-track mind.

Railroaded

Inspired by Charles Wilkes' explorations of Puget Sound, Asa Whitney, a New York trader with experience in "the Orient," petitioned Congress in 1845 for a charter to lay tracks between Lake Superior and Puget Sound. He envisioned a "grand highway to Civilize and Christianize all Mankind," not to mention haul freight between the Pacific and the Great Lakes.

A skeptical federal government did not act until the early 1850s, when the Army dispatched surveyors including future Washington Territorial Governor Isaac Stevens to scout possible routes. The Civil War shifted the focus south to plans for the Union Pacific Railroad (completed in 1869), but Congress chartered the Northern Pacific line in 1864 and provided generous land grants along its right-of-way to lure private capital. Jay Cooke responded and began pushing rails westward from Minnesota in 1870.

This news galvanized every town and village on Puget Sound, each of which vied for the honor (and certain wealth) of serving as the Northern Pacific's western terminus. From the outset, the smart money bet on Seattle — dubbed the

Northern Pacific Railroad announces selection of Tacoma for its Puget Sound terminus on July 14, 1873.

Mount Rainier spews steam and ash on October 19, 1873.

Coal gas lights Seattle streets, homes, and businesses for the first time on December 31, 1873.

Scheduled steamship service commences between Seattle and San Francisco on March 3, 1875.

Seattle citizens begin work on their own railroad, the Seattle & Walla Walla, on May 1, 1874.

Dexter Horton

"Queen City of the Pacific Northwest" by Portland real estate promoters — which triggered a wave of speculation and the city's first East Coast investments.

Seattle citizens feted Northern Pacific officials and surveyors and offered a generous bounty of land and cash to win the terminus. The city also had the advantage of ample soft coal from new mines near Newcastle. Imagine, then, the crowd's shocked reaction on July 14, 1873, when Arthur Denny publicly read this telegram from Northern Pacific: "We have located the terminus on Commencement Bay."

Mayor Bailey Gatzert

Coal and Steel

Tacoma had been anointed "the city of destiny" chiefly because the NP had bought up all the prime real estate, but Jay Cooke's financial empire collapsed soon after. Meanwhile, on May 1, 1874, virtually every able-bodied male in the town showed up near present-day Georgetown and began grading for a locally financed Seattle & Walla Walla Railroad.

After this initial burst of "Seattle Spirit" volunteer enthusiasm, Chinese immigrants took over the real work under the direction of Scottish-born engineer James M. Colman.

Seattle & Walla Walla tracks never reached the railroad's last namesake city, but they did link Seattle with the coal mines of Newcastle, and a generous municipal franchise gave it exclusive access to the growing downtown waterfront. Seattle had a short but profitable railway by 1878 while Tacoma languished waiting for construction of the Northern Pacific to resume.

Thus, Seattle turned reversal into

A Shakespeare play, *The Taming of the Shrew*, is performed for the first time in Seattle on March 15, 1875.

Seattle elects its first Jewish mayor, Bailey Gatzert, on August 2, 1875.

City of Seattle buys land that becomes Volunteer Park in 1876.

Scandinavian Immigration and Aid Society is formed in Seattle in 1876.

Two Wheels Are Better Than None

On November 14, 1879, the first bicycle ever seen in Washington Territory arrived aboard a steamer from San Francisco via Portland. Seattle Merchant William H. Pumphrey displayed the boy's size two-wheeler in front of his store at 617 Front Street (later 1st Avenue). Jules Lipsky bought the bicycle for his son four days later.

Georgetown's first breweries opened in late 1870s

progress. The population grew and diversified with new arrivals from Europe and Asia, community services expanded, new institutions such as the Sisters of Providence downtown hospital sprang up, women took an increasingly influential role in politics and civic development, and a self-reliant economy now chiefly fueled by coal and regional and Pacific shipping firmly established itself.

Seattle's population tripled to 3,533 during the decade and ranked second in the territory to Walla Walla by a scant 50 residents when President Rutherford B. Hayes visited the Queen City and its nearby coal mines on October 11, 1880. Destiny, it seemed, had favored Seattle after all.

Clara McCarty receives the University of Washington's first baccalaureate degree in July 1876.

Seattle YMCA is organized on August 7, 1876.

Sisters of Providence begin operating the King County Hospital in Georgetown in May 1877.

First white criminal to be legally executed in Washington is hanged in Renton on September 28, 1877.

Seattle's first telephone and phonograph are demonstrated in 1878 and Georgetown starts brewing beer.

Sisters of Providence open Seattle's first hospital on August 2, 1878.

Seattle's first bicycle arrives from San Francisco on November 14, 1879.

Squire's Opera House, Seattle's first true theater, opens on November 24, 1879.

U.S. President Rutherford B. Hayes visits Seattle, Renton, and Newcastle on October 11, 1880, during first presidential tour west of the Rockies.

Seattle waterfront during "big snow" of 1880.
Below: Early telephone

Seattle's first train hauled coal from Lake Union to Pike Street in 1872

SISTERHOOD IS POWERFUL, PART I

The great feminist and abolitionist Susan B. Anthony paid the first of two visits to Seattle in October 1871 and helped organize the Washington Equal Suffrage Association with local advocates such as Sarah Yesler. Women would gain and lose the vote in Seattle and Washington several times before passage of a state constitutional suffrage amendment in 1910 — a decade before ratification of the 19th Amendment to the U.S. Constitution. Long before they gained the vote, many women assumed leadership positions in education, social reform, labor organizing, and other spheres of civic life.

SISTERHOOD IS POWERFUL, PART II

The Sisters of Charity of Providence arrived in Seattle in 1877 to manage the King County Hospital in Georgetown. Self-trained architect and contractor Mother Joseph, born Esther Pariseau, supervised construction of Seattle's first true hospital. The three-story structure opened August 2, 1878, at 5th Avenue and Madison Street, on the present site of the Federal Courthouse. The structure was succeeded by a larger hospital, designed by Donald McKay in 1882. Providence Hospital relocated to the Central Area in 1911, and ultimately merged operations with Swedish Medical Center in 2000.

Native canoes and other craft at the foot of S Washington Street
Below: A Mosquito Fleet steamer and Henry Villard

1881~1900: Golden Phoenix

Seattle consolidated its status as Puget Sound's leading city during the 1880s — and then came close to going up in smoke. Even "The Great Fire" of 1889 proved a blessing in disguise for a town that did not seem to know the meaning of the word quit.

Transportation improvements were key to the city's growing success. As the decade opened, few roads outside of the original downtown were planked or paved, and rail service remained limited. Water was the preferred medium for regional travel as an expanding swarm of "Mosquito Fleet" steamers flitted between Puget Sound ports and crisscrossed Lake Washington. Regularly scheduled ferry service would not be introduced until Christmas Eve 1888, when the West Seattle Land and Improvement Company began shuttling commuters and potential homebuyers between downtown and a dock below Duwamish Head.

Erratic rail service remained a source of economic and public frustration through much of the decade. The Northern Pacific's managers continued to favor Tacoma over Seattle until 1883, when Henry Villard took control of the railroad. He earned Seattle's trust when his Oregon Improvement Company purchased the local Seattle & Walla Walla in 1880, and the town threw him a lavish tribute when he visited in September 1883.

Thomas Burke

On that occasion, Villard promised to build a spur line between Tacoma and Seattle. It opened with great fanfare on June 17, 1884; unfortunately, Villard was ousted soon after. His successors saw no reason to foster Seattle's economy at the expense of their own Tacoma-based interests.

The unreliability of the trains running between the two cities earned the line the nickname "Orphan Road." In 1885, Judge Thomas Burke and Daniel Gilman raised capital for a new railroad, the Seattle Lake Shore & Eastern, with the ambition of linking Seattle to the new Canadian Pacific transcontinental line near Sumas. Before reaching this goal, the SLS&E laid track from downtown to Ballard and east to present-day Issaquah. The line became a major regional carrier of coal, produce, and passengers, and joggers and bicyclists can still follow much of this route on today's Burke-Gilman Trail. Ironically, the NP ended up owning both the SLS& E and the earlier Seattle & Walla Walla, and maintained an effective monopoly on Seattle rail service until the arrival of the Great Northern Railway in 1893.

Telephone exchange begins service for 90 Seattle subscribers on March 7, 1883.

Vashon Island post office opens on April 12, 1883.

Seattle's first independent charity, The Ladies Relief Society (now Seattle Children's Home), is organized on April 4, 1884.

Western Washington Women's Christian Temperance Union (WCTU) holds first annual convention in Seattle in June 1884 and launches campaign for prohibition.

Northern Pacific runs first train from Tacoma to Seattle on June 17, 1884.

Seattle's first horse-drawn streetcars begin rolling along 2nd Avenue on September 23, 1884.

FRONTIER INJUSTICE

On January 18, 1882, a mob of 200 lynched three men from a beam bridging two trees on the corner of James Street and 1st Avenue. James Sullivan and William Howard were seized in the courtroom after being arraigned for robbing and fatally wounding businessman George B. Reynolds. The mob then broke down the King County jail doors, and dragged out Benjamin Payne, a suspect in the killing of Seattle police officer David Sires on October 12, 1881. Before the mob hanged him, Payne cried out, "You hang me, and you will hang an innocent man." The board and ropes used in the lynching were left in the trees for many years as a warning to other would-be criminals.

Eyewitness sketch of 1882 lynching

Harpers Weekly sketch of 1886 anti-Chinese riot

Enumclaw is founded in 1885.

Seattle, Lake Shore & Eastern Railroad Company is incorporated on April 15, 1885.

Seattle's First African Methodist Episcopal Church is founded in 1886.

Seattle mob rounds up Chinese residents on February 7, 1886 and forces them to board a ship for San Francisco before a violent battle between white workers and police.

The first electric lightbulb to shine west of the Rockies is turned on in Seattle on March 22, 1886.

YMCA opens Seattle's first gymnasium in November 1886 and soon introduces the new game of "basket ball."

RACE RIOT

Anti-Chinese violence in King County took its first lives on September 7, 1885, when white and Indian hop pickers attacked immigrant laborers near present-day Issaquah, killing three. On February 7 of the following year, an armed mob of white workers descended on Seattle's original Chinatown centered around 3rd Avenue S and S Washington Street. They rounded up virtually all Seattle's 350 residents of Chinese birth or descent and marched them to the Ocean Pier at the foot of Main Street, where a steamer bound for San Francisco waited. Police and a volunteer "Home Guard" responded to protect the Chinese, 200 of whom departed the following morning. When they tried to return the rest to their homes, the mob rioted. Shots were fired, and five agitators fell wounded, one fatally. President Grover Cleveland and Territorial Governor Watson Squires declared martial law, and most of the city's Chinese escaped unharmed. Immigration gradually resumed and a new Chinatown took root in today's International District by 1910. The federal government compensated China because of the West Coast riots, but the actual victims never saw a cent.

Thanks But No Thanks

During the early 1880s and previous decade, more and more of the hard physical labor of laying tracks, grading roads, mining coal, canning salmon, and harvesting crops was performed by immigrants actively recruited from China through brokers such as the Seattle-based Wa Chong Company. At first, these industrious workers were welcomed by their new neighbors, and a lively Chinatown coalesced around the intersection of 3rd Avenue S and S Washington Street on the eastern fringe of present-day Pioneer Square.

Seattle & Walla Walla terminal in Pioneer Square

Chinese merchant Chin Gee Hee

Admiration turned to resentment, however, as local white and even Indian workers found themselves losing employment to growing numbers of immigrants willing — as though they had an actual choice — to accept low wages and dangerous working conditions. The displacement of local workers in turn helped to fuel the growth of the area's early labor unions, notably the Knights of Labor, and led to anti-Chinese actions in local mines as early as 1876.

An economic downturn during the mid-1880s intensified bad feelings up and down the West Coast, prompting passage of "exclusion laws" to bar Chinese ownership of property and set federal limits on further immigration. Mobs in several cities, including Seattle and Tacoma, forcibly rounded up and expelled Chinese workers in 1885 and 1886. It took two decades for Seattle's Chinese community to recover.

Sparks Fly

Electricity made its local debut during the 1880s. The first telephone exchange linked 90 "subscribers" in 1883, and the West's first light bulb was switched on in Seattle three years later. Local entrepreneurs quickly recognized that electricity could transform the landscape by harnessing it to the city's primitive, horse-drawn streetcar system. Again Seattle led the West by inaugurating the first all-electric street railway in 1889. Developers also borrowed cable car technology from San Francisco to link downtown with Lake Washington — where they built Leschi Park and a menagerie to lure riders.

Although they used public streets under government franchises, Seattle's first urban and interurban transportation systems were privately owned and operated. Their routes were often laid out to promote sales in new developments such as Ballard, Columbia City, and Georgetown, all of which were established by the end of the decade.

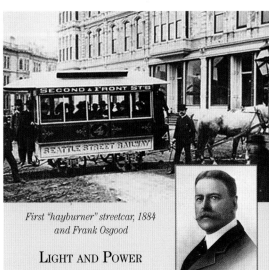

First "hayburner" streetcar, 1884 and Frank Osgood

LIGHT AND POWER

Before Seattle's first electric streetcars were tested on March 31, 1889, alarmists predicted that pocket watches would be magnetized and bolts of lightning would strike down pedestrians. System owner Frank Osgood gave investor Addie Burns the privilege of being the system's first passenger as the new cars performed flawlessly even on downtown's steep grades. Osgood retired his horse-drawn streetcars by April 5, which gave Seattle the distinction of being the first West Coast city with an all-electric street railway. By the century's end, electric traction was Seattle's primary mode of urban and interurban transportation.

British author Rudyard Kipling visited Seattle shortly after the Great Fire and described the downtown district as a "a horrible black smudge, as though a hand had come down and rubbed the place smooth."

OCCIDENTAL HOTEL

SEATTLE DAILY PRESS

FIRE STARTER

The Great Fire of 1889 was long blamed on the wrong man. Original reports in the *Seattle Post-Intelligencer* cited John McGough's cabinet shop as the point of origin and this claim was repeated in many subsequent accounts. Decades later, historian James Warren discovered a correction published on June 21, 1889, which shifted blame to the adjacent Clairmont shop. In the article, John A. Back, a newly arrived cabinetmaker from Sweden, explained in detail how he had lost control of the overheated glue that ignited the blaze. For understandable reasons, Back left Seattle for San Francisco soon after and changed his name to Beck.

Above: Ruins of the Occidental Hotel. Left: Fire spreading on June 6, 1889. Right: *Post-Intelligencer*

Before the availability of an extensive system of paved roads and the automobile, street railways were essential to both urban density and suburban expansion. Indeed, modern cities owe as much to streetcars as they do to the elevators that allowed buildings to rise above a few stories.

From this point of view, downtown Seattle could not have burned down at a better time. The Great Fire of June 6, 1889, began with an overheated glue pot in a cabinet shop at 1st Avenue and Madison Street. Abetted by a hot summer and a brisk wind, the flames quickly leapt from one wood-framed building to the next.

Volunteer firefighters and citizens tapped into the town's privately-owned water supply and found barely a trickle. By sunset, 64 acres lay in smoking ruins. British author Rudyard Kipling visited a few weeks later during a Puget Sound lecture tour and described the downtown district as a "a horrible black smudge, as though a Hand had come down and rubbed the place smooth. I know now what being wiped out means."

YMCA Hoopsters

Reform and Reconstruction

First Cedar River power plant

In truth, Seattle was down but far from out. The fire had wiped the frontier slate clean and allowed the city to rebuild itself as a modern urban center — with stone and brick, not wood. Planners also took the opportunity to elevate downtown's flood-prone streets a full story, stranding the ground floors of some buildings and creating the route of today's "Underground Tour" in Pioneer Square.

Politics also took a modern turn under Mayor Robert Moran, a reformist engineer and ship builder. Advocates of municipal ownership of utilities scored their first great victory a month after the fire when voters, still simmering from the failure of private water supplies, overwhelmingly approved development of a public water supply on the Cedar River.

Robert Moran

Effective February 8, 1887, the Dawes Severalty Act subdivides Indian reservations and intensifies federal efforts to "civilize" Native American cultures.

Seattle's first cable cars enter service between Pioneer Square and Leschi on September 28, 1887.

Rainier Club is established on February 23, 1888.

Territorial Supreme Court declares women's suffrage unconstitutional in Nevada Bloomer case on August 14, 1888.

Puget Sound's first scheduled ferry service begins with a run between Seattle and West Seattle on December 24, 1888.

First electric streetcars run on March 31, 1889.

"The Great Fire" scorches 64 acres of downtown Seattle on June 6, 1889.

On July 8, 1889, Seattle voters approve construction of city-owned Cedar River water system.

VICE VS. VIRTUE

In February 1888, Madame Lou Graham arrived in Seattle and quickly founded the city's most sumptuous, lucrative, and expensive house of prostitution. She established the house in downtown Seattle at 3rd Avenue S and S Washington Street, and it was frequented by Seattle's most elite business leaders and visitors. Next door stood the city's first Catholic church, Our Lady of Good Help, which prompted one pioneer to marvel that you could find "piety and prostitution on the same corner." Graham made a fortune before dying in 1903 at age 43 of an occupational disease: syphilis. Our Lady of Good Help was torn down the following year, but the building that housed Graham's bordello still survives.

Washington becomes the 42nd state of the Union on November 11, 1889.

Steamboat *C. C. Calkins* starts regular run between Seattle and East Seattle (Mercer Island) on March 21, 1890.

Seattle beats Spokane 11 to 8 in the city's first professional baseball game, played at Madison Park on May 24, 1890.

The city also introduced standardized "Australian Ballots" in 1890, which greatly reduced election fraud. For at least half the population, however, the single most important reform remained elusive. Women were granted the right to vote by the Territorial Legislature in 1883, but suffrage was voided by the Supreme Court three years later. The Legislature restored the ballot in 1888, and the Court annulled it a month later. Male voters rejected a woman suffrage plank in the proposed state constitution in 1889, but women regained the right to vote in school elections the following year. This battle of the sexes became increasingly entangled in the debate over prohibition and would drag on two more decades.

In 1890, Ballard was incorporated and named for developer Capt. William Rankin Ballard, and newly platted Georgetown was named for the grandson of pioneer banker Dexter Horton. Seattle hummed with new projects and prospects, and attracted 10,000 new residents within one year of The Great Fire. It ended the decade with a population of 42,000 and King County counted a total of 63,000 — a growth of nearly tenfold that established both city and county as the largest in the brand new State of Washington.

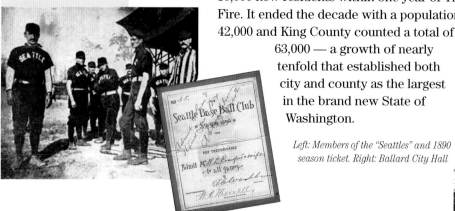

Left: Members of the "Seattles" and 1890 season ticket. Right: Ballard City Hall

Territorial Ambitions

Charles Dickens' famous epigram, "It was the best of times, it was the worst of times," would resonate profoundly for Seattle during the final decade of the 19th century. While still rebuilding from the Great Fire, Seattle finally realized its dream of a direct transcontinental railway link with the arrival of the Great Northern in 1893. Then it plunged headlong into a deep depression triggered by that year's national economic "Panic." Recovery arrived unexpectedly and dramatically four years later aboard a steamer laden with gold from the Klondike River, securing the city new international prominence and unprecedented prosperity.

The decade began on a positive note with Seattle's annexation of northern neighborhoods including Magnolia, Wallingford, Fremont, Green Lake, Brooklyn (now the University District), and Ravenna. The vote more than doubled Seattle's land area to a total of almost 30 square miles and added thousands of new residents.

Development of these areas was already accelerating thanks to the construction of new railroads, streetcar lines, and bridges. Similarly, new interurban railways linking Seattle with Georgetown and Renton spurred new industry, agriculture, and housing on the city's southeastern flank during the early 1890s, although this area would not formally join the city until 1907.

The biggest news of the decade's early years was the steady advance of James J. Hill's Great Northern Railway westward from Minnesota and across the Cascades, and then south from Everett. Hill selected Seattle as his terminus despite the fact that the rival Northern Pacific had a stranglehold on the city's central waterfront thanks to its purchase of the lucrative franchises previously granted to local railroads. For the time being, Hill's tracks terminated at a giant pier (forerunner of Piers 90-91) on Smith's Cove, where his Pacific steamships later transfered cargo to high-speed "silk trains" bound for East Coast mills.

Guy Phinney begins running streecars between Fremont and his Woodland Park estate and menagerie in 1890.

In August 1890, Isaac W. Evans becomes the first African American appointed to the Seattle police force.

First cargo of wheat is shipped from Seattle on November 3, 1890.

Women's Century Club is founded in 1891.

Seattle Seminary — later Seattle Pacific University — opens doors to 34 students on April 4, 1891.

Annexation of Magnolia, Wallingford, Green Lake, and University District neighborhoods doubles Seattle's size on May 3, 1891.

U.S. President Benjamin Harrison visits Seattle on May 6, 1891.

Latona Bridge across Lake Union is dedicated on July 1, 1891. (A trestle to Fremont is completed the next year.)

Sarah Bernhardt performs in Seattle on September 24, 1891.

Early Green Lake scene with streetcar

Furuya Company is founded in Seattle's new "Japan Town" (now the International District) in 1892.

Midget Mrs. Tom Thumb arrives in Seattle for four performances on June 23 and 24, 1892.

Northup Post Office opens in present-day Bellevue on July 29, 1892.

B. F. Day Elementary School (Seattle's oldest extant school) opens in Fremont in September 1892.

Congregation Ohaveth Sholom opens Washington's first synagogue on September 18, 1892.

First train robbery in Washington occurs on November 24, 1892.

Great Northern Railway drives in last spike to complete a direct transcontinental line to Seattle on January 6, 1893.

Panic in the Streets

The Great Northern's last spike was driven on January 6, 1893, but the celebration was short-lived. Revelations that the nation's gold reserves were nearly depleted and a series of high-profile bankruptcies toppled the stock market the following May and triggered an economic "Panic" that would persist four years.

The national depression hit Seattle and other capital-hungry western cities especially hard. Among the early casualties were Peter Kirk's dream of turning his namesake town on Lake Washington into the "Pittsburgh of the West" and pioneer David T. Denny's plans for development of the communities adjacent to the University of Washington's new campus on Portage Bay. Another ambitious developer, Guy Phinney, died in 1893 and saddled his widow Nellie with debt and a 200-acre "Woodland Park" estate that she would ultimately sell to the City of Seattle in 1899.

Workers suffered along with capitalists, and more than 650 unemployed men from Seattle joined Jacob Coxey's "army" in a march to Washington D.C., to demand federal relief in April 1894. The depression also fueled the growth of local labor unions, which had been steadily multiplying and gaining members, including many European immigrants, over the past decade.

New post-fire buildings at 3rd and Cherry

Early Seattle annexations

Despite hard times, economic progress did not halt entirely. If East Coast financing was not available, the city could still look to the Far East for trade to help fill the void. James Hill arranged for Seattle's selection as the first U.S. port of call for regular Japanese shipping. Seattle greeted the steamship *Miiki Maru* with a grateful clamor of church bells and factory whistles as she docked on August 31, 1896. The ensuing commerce and a growing influx of immigrants would promote a new "Japan Town" with its own churches, businesses, and newspapers in today's International District.

31

Equality for Some

Seattle's social progress was uneven, however. Its established African American communities gained acceptance and founded new institutions such as the Mount Zion Baptist Church, but the recruitment of Southern black coal miners to break strikes and weaken unions antagonized other workers. In reaction, the state gutted its pioneering 1890 law guaranteeing equal access to public accommodations and services.

The growing power of political Populists, who swept the 1896 elections, would prove a mixed blessing for many racial and ethnic minorities due to lingering white worker resentments of immigrant and non-union labor. The movement for universal suffrage also stalled during the decade, but women were active on other fronts, establishing new institutions such as a Seattle branch of the YWCA and the Women's Century Club (whose Capitol Hill headquarters now houses the Harvard Exit Theater).

Town of Slaughter is renamed Auburn on February 21, 1893.

National economic "Panic of 1893" sends King County into a four year depression on May 5, 1893.

Telephone service between Seattle, Portland, and Spokane is established on October 16, 1893.

First Seattle branch of the Young Women's Christian Association is founded on February 17, 1894.

Mount Zion Baptist Church organizes on February 18, 1894.

Coal mine fire at Franklin suffocates 37 miners on August 25, 1894.

Jesuits dedicate new Parish and School of the Immaculate Conception, now Seattle University's Garrand Building, on December 8, 1894.

Carrie Chapman Catt

THE CASE OF THE PURLOINED POLE

On October 18, 1899, town leaders proudly unveiled a 60-foot totem pole from Fort Tongass, Alaska, in Pioneer Place at the intersection of 1st Avenue and Yesler Way. It had actually been stolen from a Tlingit village several weeks before by acting Chamber of Commerce president James Clise and 14 other business leaders while returning from a "good will tour" of Alaska sponsored by the *Seattle Post-Intelligencer*. The pole's original owners demanded $20,000 in compensation and a federal grand jury indicted eight prominent totem-takers for theft of government property (since the Tlingits lived on public land). The case was thrown out but the *P-I* paid the Tlingits $500 token recompense. The original totem was seriously damaged in an arson fire on October 22, 1938. The federal government paid descendents of the first pole's sculptors to carve a replacement, which was installed in 1940.

Club co-founder Carrie Chapman Catt would succeed Susan B. Anthony as the national standard bearer for woman suffrage by the decade's close.

Anti-Catholic propaganda increased during the decade, but anti-semitism had not yet appeared on any significant scale as Seattle's small but influential Jewish community grew and diversified. Chevra Bikur Cholim was organized in 1891 to care for the sick, and Ohaveth Sholom built the state's first synagogue the following year. The congregation later divided over doctrinal issues and reform Jews coalesced as Temple de Hirsch in 1899. They erected a new synagogue two years later.

School Days

After much delay, the University of Washington relocated from downtown Seattle to a wooded tract long reserved for it on the north shore of Portage Bay. Its first building, today's Denny Hall, welcomed students in the fall of 1895.

The UW would soon have competition. In 1891, Free Method-

A PRINCESS PASSES

On May 31, 1896, Suquamish Princess Angeline died at the age of 76 in her waterfront shack located on Western Avenue between Pike and Pine streets. The eldest daughter of Seattle and his first wife, she was named Kick-is-om-lo Seattle. She married Dokub Cud, who died before the arrival of Euro-American settlers on Puget Sound. When pioneer Catherine Maynard heard the name, she announced, "You are too good looking a woman to carry around such a name as that, and I now christen you Angeline." At her request, Angeline was buried near her old friend, pioneer Henry Yesler, in Lake View Cemetery.

ists founded a seminary on the north slope of Queen Anne Hill that would become Seattle Pacific University, while two Jesuit priests arrived that fall to begin teaching Catholic boys. In 1894, they established a new parish and school on the present-day campus of Seattle University. Meanwhile, Seattle's public school district launched an aggressive construction program to meet the needs of the city's newly annexed neighborhoods.

The YMCA pursued innovations in education and recreation, introducing Seattle to basketball in 1893 and setting up the city's first vocational school in 1899. The Y filled an important gap in social services and education, especially in serving teens and immigrants, but its increasingly secular mission alienated conservative founders such as Dexter Horton.

Original UW columns now form a "Sylvan Theater"

FORE!

In 1895, the game of golf arrived in Seattle when 12 prominent citizens, including Josiah Collins, E. A. Strout, and James "Gillie" Gillium, played a round in a borrowed Wallingford pasture near the north shore of Lake Union. The primitive course had five short holes laid out along what would later become Stone Way N. Greens and tees were maintained with a hand mower and dairy cattle grazed in the fairways. The clubhouse was a tent. In 1900, Collins formed the Seattle Golf and Country Club with 53 members. They rented 55 acres of farmland in Laurelhurst and retained professional golfer John Ball to design a 9-hole course. The club moved to The Highlands, four miles north of Ballard, in 1907 and was renamed The Seattle Golf Club.

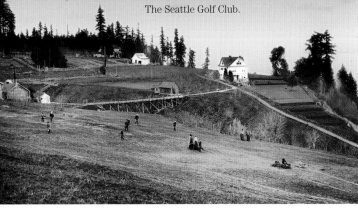

YMCA establishes Seattle's first vocational school in 1899.

Seattle's Japanese Baptist Church and first Japanese-language newspaper, *The Report*, are founded in 1899.

First phase of the Denny Regrade is completed on January 6, 1899.

Town of Gilman adopts new name of Issaquah on February 2, 1899.

Mount Rainier National Park is created on March 2, 1899.

Temple de Hirsch is founded on May 29, 1899.

Philippine trade begins in September 1899.

First cans of Carnation condensed milk processed in Kent on September 6, 1899.

Golden Fleece

Seattle awoke to a new era at 6 a.m. on the morning of July 17, 1897, when the steamship *Portland* tied up to Schwabacher's Wharf (now Waterfront Park). Alerted by reports from an enterprising *Seattle P-I* reporter named Erastus Brainerd, 5,000 spectators greeted 68 newly rich prospectors and their cargo of "more than a ton of solid gold" carved and panned from the banks of the Klondike River.

Hundreds quit their jobs that very day — including Seattle mayor William D. Wood — and began packing for the Yukon. Brainerd was hired by the Chamber of Commerce to secure Seattle's mantle as "The Gateway to Alaska" by lobbying for a government assay office and conducting a national public relations blitz. Soon, thousands of eager "sourdoughs" crowded Seattle's streets and stores, amassing supplies for the harsh gold fields of Alaska and Canada's Yukon Territory.

Few would strike it rich, but Seattle's business community prospered by picking miners' pockets to and from the Klondike. Entrepreneurs such as Robert Moran and Joshua Green made fortunes building and operating flotillas of ships to shuttle between Alaska and Puget Sound, while impresarios such as Alexander Pantages and John Cort founded vaudeville empires to entertain the bored multitudes.

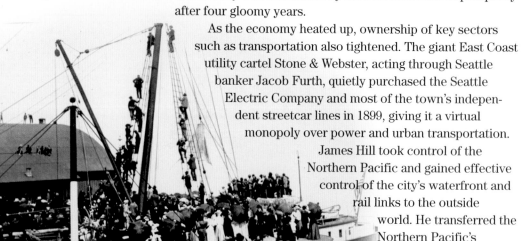

War with Spain in 1898 generated yet more wealth and established the Philippines as Seattle's newest Pacific trading partner and, later, source of a new wave of immigrants. Rail traffic expanded, real estate prices soared, and construction resumed; no sphere of economic or social activity was untouched by the sudden return of prosperity after four gloomy years.

As the economy heated up, ownership of key sectors such as transportation also tightened. The giant East Coast utility cartel Stone & Webster, acting through Seattle banker Jacob Furth, quietly purchased the Seattle Electric Company and most of the town's independent streetcar lines in 1899, giving it a virtual monopoly over power and urban transportation. James Hill took control of the Northern Pacific and gained effective control of the city's waterfront and rail links to the outside world. He transferred the Northern Pacific's

900,000 acres of forested land grant holdings to George Weyerhaeuser, an old friend from Minnesota, in one of the largest real estate transactions in U.S. history.

Local populists, progressives, labor organizers, and government reformers of all political persuasions were alarmed by the rapid consolidation of economic power in so few hands. The lines were now drawn in a political and economic war that would rage for much of the next century — and still reverberates in today's battles over deregulation and globalization.

Early Pantages Theater

THEY COME, THEY GO...

Seattle attracted a growing parade of famous visitors and entertainers during the 1890s, starting with U.S. President Benjamin Harrison in 1891. Later that year, actress Sarah Bernhardt (center) performed in town and then went hunting on Guy Phinney's (left) Woodland Park estate (below). The diminutive Mrs. Tom Thumb entertained in 1892, and author Mark Twain's (right) 1895 lecture elicited "one continuous laugh" from sell-out crowds according to a *P-I* review.

Populist orator and presidential candidate William Jennings Bryan divided the house during his April 1900 campaign visit. The Democratic-leaning *Seattle Times* judged The Great Commoner's tour a tremendous success and the then-Republican *P-I* declared it a "failure." Despite the state's populist sympathies, Bryan lost Washington and the national election to McKinley that fall.

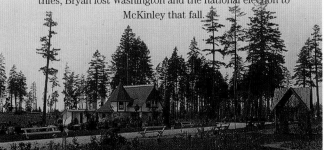

Town fathers proudly unveil a stolen Tlingit totem pole in Pioneer Square on October 18, 1899.

City of Seattle purchases Woodland Park and its menagerie on December 28, 1899.

Local banker Jacob Furth, acting for Boston-based utility cartel Stone & Webster, acquires Seattle Electric Company and most streetcar lines in 1899.

Being able to count, Seattle residents do NOT celebrate the eve of the 20th century on December 31, 1899.

James Hill takes control of Northern Pacific Railway and sells its 900,000 acres of forested land grant property to Frederick Weyerhaeuser on January 3, 1900.

U.S. Army establishes Fort Lawton in Magnolia on February 9, 1900.

King County's first automobile (an electric model) arrives on July 23, 1900.

Downtown Carnegie Library

1901~1920:
High and Dry

The new century began in Seattle with a book burning — perhaps intentional — as the Seattle Public Library and its home in the Yesler Mansion (on the present site of the King County Courthouse) were reduced to ashes. Authorities ruled it arson, and many suspected city librarian Charles Wesley Smith, but no culprit was ever named.

Regardless, Smith reapplied for financial aid to steel-magnate-turned-philanthropist Andrew Carnegie, who had previously dismissed Seattle as a "hot air boom town." This time, Carnegie responded with funds for a new downtown library and several neighborhood branches, most of which survive today.

Fire — and Klondike gold— it seemed, had cast a magic spell on Seattle. The town's population grew by an astounding 25,000 in the final three years of the 19th century to top 80,000. King County numbered more than 110,000 residents.

Power Plays

Civic leaders, especially those with a progressive or reformist bent, were quick to seize the political agenda. Fearing the private monopoly over electric power and street railways, municipal ownership advocates such as City

Timeline

Seattle Public Library burns down on January 1, 1901.

Bellevue's first church (Congregational) is established in 1901.

Village of Kenmore is named on January 10, 1901.

Temple de Hirsch cornerstone is laid on June 9, 1901.

Developer James Moore names Seattle's Capitol Hill in the fall of 1901.

Seattle's first Sephardic Jews arrive in 1902.

Broadway High School, Seattle's first dedicated high school, opens in 1902.

Seattle voters approve electric utility bonds on March 4, 1902, leading to creation of Seattle City Light.

Escaped desperado Harry Tracy terrorizes King County in July 1902 and kills three policemen before being gunned down near Spokane on August 5.

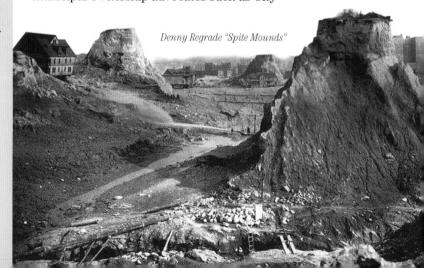

Denny Regrade "Spite Mounds"

Fremont-Green Lake steetcar

Engineer Reginald H. Thomson successfully persuaded Seattle's voters in 1902 to fund development of a hydroelectric power plant in the new public watershed on the Cedar River. Guided by young engineer James D. Ross, the turbines were lighting Seattle streets by January 1905 and soon began competing with archrival Seattle Electric (a forerunner of today's Puget Sound Energy) for commercial and residential customers.

Meanwhile, Seattle Electric's parent holding company, Stone & Webster, continued amassing control of electric-powered transportation. It completed an interurban line to Tacoma in 1902 and pushed a line to Everett in 1910. A link was later added between Mount Vernon and Bellingham, but the company never realized its vision of a seamless electric railway running from Vancouver to Vancouver.

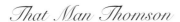

That Man Thomson

The new prosperity revived the race for prime real estate, and James A. Moore grabbed the high ground. He finished the huge but derelict hotel begun by Arthur Denny atop his namesake hill, renamed it the Washington Hotel, and handed the first guest room keys to U.S. President Theodore Roosevelt on May 3, 1903.

City Engineer R.H. Thomson was not impressed. He

J.D. Ross

loathed Denny Hill's steep escarpment along Pine Street as an obstacle to Seattle's "natural" expansion northward and ached to flatten it. He had already begun nibbling at its western Belltown slopes, but Moore refused to surrender. The two finally reached an accommodation: Thomson could have the hill when Moore finished his adjacent namesake

Interurban rail service begins between Seattle and Tacoma on September 25, 1902.

John Olmsted arrives in Seattle to design city parks in April 1903.

U.S. President Theodore Roosevelt visits Seattle and Fort Lawton on May 23, 1903.

Seattle Symphony Orchestra performs its first concert on December 29, 1903.

Alaska Building, Seattle's first steel-framed skyscraper, is completed in 1904.

Georgetown incorporates as a city on January 8, 1904.

Moran Brothers Shipyard launches USS Battleship *Nebraska*, partially subsidized by Seattle citizens, on October 7, 1904.

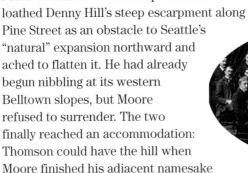

First Seattle Symphony players

Washington Hotel ca. 1902

hotel and a New Washington Hotel (now the Josephinum) to replace Denny's Victorian pile. This done, Thomson's workers dumped and sluiced 5 million cubic yards of soil into Elliott Bay to create today's Denny Regrade.

Thomson did not limit his digging to Denny Hill and its northern slopes. He attacked most of downtown, leveling the former Territorial University campus on Denny Knoll and, later, Jackson Street and today's International District. Much of the fill was used to elevate Seattle's future industrial district and rail yards on the vast mud flats south of Pioneer Square. The spoils of Eugene Semple's aborted attempt to dig a canal between Elliott Bay and Lake Washington through Beacon Hill and Duwamish River dredging were used to create the Port of Seattle.

R.H. Thomson

Reaching for the Sky

Amid all of this earthmoving, Seattle's skyline began to rise to new heights thanks to the new technology of steel-frame construction. The Alaska Building debuted as the city's first "skyscraper" in 1904 and was quickly followed by the Hoge Building, Frye Hotel, and Moore's New Washington Hotel. Other major new downtown buildings included a grand new Post Office and the Carnegie Library.

By now, the downtown's retail and financial core had begun to migrate north from Pioneer Square thanks to Thomson's regrades. The University of Washington left its original campus and Regents tried in vain to sell or develop the prime eight-block "Metropolitan Tract." Finally in 1907, a new group of investors led by James Douglas organized the Metropolitan Building

Alaska Building

Company to construct an ensemble of modern and successful office buildings, including the surviving Cobb Building at 4th Avenue and University and later Skinner Building. Today's Unico Properties manages the tract in trust for its UW owners nearly a century later.

Also in 1907, consumers and local farmers rebelled against the economic tyranny of grocery middlemen. City Council Member Thomas Revelle won approval of a Saturday "public market" at the foot of Pike Street, and prospector-turned-developer Frank Goodwin began building an ensemble of permanent stalls and arcades which remain the heart of today's Pike Place Public Market.

In 1907, the city's land area doubled again with the annexation of West Seattle, Ballard, and most of Southeast Seattle except Georgetown, which held out until 1910. (Seattle pushed north to 145th Street with its final round of annex-

World's Longest Tunnel

In 1903, City Engineer R.H. Thomson prevailed on James J. Hill, who then controlled both the Great Northern and Northern Pacific railroads, not to compound the dangerous congestion on the "Railroad Avenue" that lined the central waterfront. Instead, Hill dug a tunnel beneath downtown to the site of his new King Street Station (left), completed in 1906. Workers joked that it was the world's longest tunnel since it ran "from Virginia to Washington" — streets, that is. The Union Pacific added its own grand depot, Union Station, in 1911 to serve its trains and those of the Milwaukee Road.

Children's Orthopedic Hospital is founded in early 1907.

Seattle annexes six towns including Ballard and West Seattle in 1907.

America's first gas station opens in Seattle in 1907.

Pike Place Market opens on August 17, 1907.

American Messenger Service, now UPS, begins operating from a Pioneer Square saloon on August 28, 1907.

Pike Place Market ca. 1910

Early Volunteer and Frink Park views

THE OLMSTED LEGACY

Seattle's Parks Department retained the famed Olmsted Brothers (Frederick Law Jr., and John C., son and stepson of New York Grand Central Park creator Frederick Law Olmsted) to design a comprehensive park system in 1903. John C. Olmsted returned after the 1907 annexations and consulted on Seattle parks until 1940. Among the Olmsted legacies in Seattle are Lake Washington Boulevard, Seward Park, Woodland Park, Volunteer Park, and the Washington Park Aboretum.

James Moore hired Olmsted to design his "Millionaire's Row" subdivision south of Volunteer Park on Capitol Hill (which Moore named in 1900). Olmsted also directed initial planning for the new University of Washington campus, which would host Seattle's first world's fair in 1909.

John C. Olmsted

Thomas A. Edison visits Seattle on September 11, 1908.

Seattle's first Italian and Slavic language newspapers are published in 1908 and 1909 respectively.

Alaska-Yukon-Pacific Exposition opens for a 138 day run on June 1, 1909.

Luna Park

ations in 1954.) Meanwhile, visionary Seattle schools superintendent Frank Cooper launched an ambitious program of construction, including the city's first high school in 1902, and classroom innovations to serve thousands of new students.

Time To Party

When not learning or earning, Seattle citizens could enjoy themselves in the city's expanding parks system, planned by the Olmsted Brothers beginning in 1903, and at amusement centers such as West Seattle's Luna Park. The biggest attraction of the decade was the Alaska-Yukon-Pacific Exposition, or A-Y-P for short, on the University of Washington's new campus. The A-Y-P had originally been planned to mark the tenth anniversary of the Klondike Gold Rush, but a national recession in 1907 delayed its execution. The event opened almost two years late on June 1, 1909 and ran through October 16.

As Seattle's international profile rose, it also became

SOUVENIR TICKET
Alaska-Yukon-Pacific Exposition
SEATTLE DAY SEPTEMBER 6TH
A.D. Barrell
CHIEF OF ADMISSIONS
J.E. Chilberg
PRESIDENT

SEATTLE'S FIRST WORLD'S FAIR

On June 1, 1909 at 8 a.m. the gates opened for the 138-day run of the Alaska-Yukon-Pacific Exposition on the University of Washington campus in Seattle. Just moments before 12 noon Pacific time, President William Howard Taft pressed a telegraph key made from Klondike gold nuggets. The signal raced across the continent from the White House to ring a gong at the fairgrounds and set off a deafening cacophony of whistles and horns from businesses throughout Seattle. The A-Y-P included hundreds of local and international exhibits housed in elegant buildings, along with fountains and formal gardens in the style of Versailles, laid out with a panoramic view of Mount Rainier. The A-Y-P was also the terminus for the nation's first transcontinental automobile race and featured balloon ascensions and a primitive Zeppelin. Over the fair's 138 days, 3,140,551 persons attended at a cost of 50 cents each (two bits for kids). Surviving vestiges of the A-Y-P include the UW's Drumheller Fountain, Cunningham Building, and original Architecture Hall, and Pioneer Square's ornate Pergola, which was built over an elaborate public restroom to serve fair-bound streetcar passengers.

TRAVELING 1,250,000 MILES
CARRYING 3,000,000 PASSENGERS
25,000 FLIGHTS
VISITORS TO THE ALASKA YUKON PACIFIC EXPOSITION
FLY ON THE FLYER
BETWEEN SEATTLE AND TACOMA

GENERAL GROUND PLAN
ALASKA-YUKON-PACIFIC EXPOSITION
June 1, to Oct. 16, 1909.

Suffragists campaign for the vote, 1910

Nation's first transcontinental automobile race ends in Seattle on June 23, 1909.

African American "Buffalo Soldiers" are stationed at Fort Lawton in 1909.

Jews from Turkey incorporate Congregation Bikur Cholim, Sephardic, in 1910.

Train disaster at Wellington kills 96 on March 1, 1910.

Charles Hamilton demonstrates the first airplane in Seattle on March 11, 1910.

BUFFALO SOLDIERS

On October 9, 1909, 900 men of the U.S. Army's 25th Infantry Regiment were transferred from the Philippines to Fort Lawton (in what will become Discovery Park). The 25th is one of four regiments of African American soldiers in the Army, called "Buffalo Soldiers" by Plains Indians in the 1870s and 1880s. The soldiers and their families constituted approximately one-third of Seattle's African American population (about 2400 persons in 1910) during their stay. They were not welcomed by many of their white neighbors, and trooper Nathaniel Bledser was convicted of attempted sexual assault on dubious charges. (Photo courtesy Anthony Powell)

more socially and culturally diverse with the steady influx of immigrants — including the city's first Sephardic Jews — and racial minorities from within the United States. Organized labor also gained new numbers and confidence, and unions carried out a series of increasingly more ambitious strikes and organizing actions.

Women scored their greatest victory in 1910 when the state's all-male electorate finally granted them the right to vote on November 8. The addition of tens of thousands of mostly reform-minded women voters heartened local progressives, populists, socialists, and prohibitionists — each of whom saw the coming decade as the moment of truth for their respective, sometimes common, causes.

Kirkland voters had the honor of electing the state's first woman to office when they put Carrie Shumway on the city council in 1911. Seattle voters also recalled Mayor Hiram Gill, an "open town" champion, but he would make a remarkable "conversion" and return to power as a born-again reformer.

The city's good-government movement had bigger fish to fry than Gill. Their foremost goals were to break the hold of railroad and utility monopolies on Seattle's economy, and to exorcize "demon rum" from the city. They would achieve both before the decade was half done.

Locks and Docks

Advocates of public ownership scored their first great victory in 1911 with creation of the Port of Seattle. The battles for public port districts had raged over a decade, with railroads — namely James J. Hill and his local agent, Judge Thomas Burke — maneuvering to thwart reforms in the legislature and in the courts. The political tide changed dramatically with new majorities of generally liberal women voters, and King County resoundingly approved the Port of Seattle on September 5, 1911.

A key architect of the new agency was Hiram Chittenden, who arrived in Seattle in 1906 as district chief of the U.S. Army Corps of Engineers to direct the long-stalled Lake Washington Ship Canal project. He endorsed the northern route via Lake Union, and drew up a simplified plan involving a single set of locks at Salmon Bay (which had the effect of dropping Lake Washington by nine feet and stranding former shoreline properties).

Construction on the canal began in 1911, the same year Chittenden was elected as one of the Port's first three Commissioners, and finished six years later. Arctic explorer Admiral Robert Peary's flagship led a triumphant flotilla through the new Government Locks on July 4, 1917. Chittenden, for whom the locks are now named, died a few months later. The entire waterway was not declared complete until 1934 — a mere 80 years after Thomas Mercer first floated the idea for the canal.

Army Engineer Hiram M. Chittenden

Social Engineering

This period might be summed up as "The Decade of the Engineer." In addition to Chittenden, men such as city engineer R.H. Thomson, his former aide and later Mayor George Cotterill, and City Light superintendent J.D. Ross led the charge to transform the region's physical, political, and social landscape.

Georgetown votes to annex to Seattle on March 29, 1910.

Seattle City Light becomes an independent department on April 1, 1910.

Interurban rail service between Everett and Seattle begins on April 30, 1910.

Reformers organize Municipal League of Seattle on May 23, 1910.

Women in Washington state win the vote on November 8, 1910.

Building the Ballard Locks, ca. 1916

Mayor Hiram Gill

Chlorination of Seattle
water supply begins in
1911.

Carrie Shumway is elected
to Kirkland City Council,
first woman so elected, in
1911.

Voters recall Mayor Hiram
Gill from office on
February 7, 1911.

Thomson's most visible impact was the methodical leveling of Denny Hill by 1911, which created a blank slate on which to sketch visions of a new city. To this end, Seattle voters approved a Municipal Plans Commission in 1910, which in turn hired architect-engineer Virgil Bogue to draw up the city's first comprehensive plan. His grand scheme for a dramatic Civic Center in the Regrade alarmed downtown property owners, and taxpayers feared its potential cost. In a rare defeat for reformers, Seattle voters rejected the Bogue Plan in 1912.

Meanwhile, City Light and the forerunner of today's Puget Sound Energy battled for customers and political advantage. J.D. Ross scored a coup in 1917 when he snatched up a federal license to tap the hydroelectric potential of the Upper Skagit River, although the first juice from Diablo Dam would not flow for another seven years.

Erecting the Smith Tower, 1914

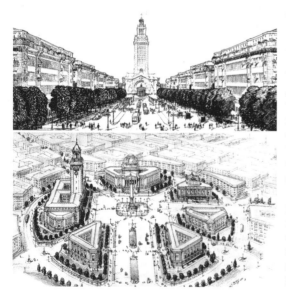

Too Far-Sighted?

In 1910, city voters approved a Municipal Plans Commission which in turn hired architect-engineer Virgil Bogue to draw up a comprehensive scheme to guide Seattle's future development. His 1911 proposal was nothing if not ambitious. It called for redevelopment of the waterfront, a system of broad boulevards, expanded streetcar lines and a rapid transit tunnel under Lake Washington, and new buildings such as Grand Central Station (top) at South Lake Union and an ornate new Civic Center in the Denny Regrade (bottom). His most audacious suggestion was to purchase Mercer Island (then largely uninhabited) for a regional park. Established property interests opposed shifting the center of downtown so far north, and ordinary taxpayers feared the plan's undisclosed cost. The "Bogue Plan" failed by two to one on March 5, 1912.

Taking Wing

Seattle literally climbed to new heights with the dedication of the Smith Tower on July 4, 1914. The 42-story edifice reigned as the "tallest building west of the Mississippi" until the Space Needle took the crown in 1962 (a Las Vegas casino now claims the distinction).

More and more aeroplanes also scraped the clouds over Seattle thanks to demonstrations by daredevils such as Charles Hamilton, Silas Christofferson, and Terah Maroney. The latter gave a young Michigan-born timber baron named William E. Boeing his first airplane ride on July 4, 1915.

In a sense, Boeing never came down. In 1916, he joined with Navy Lt. Conrad Westervelt and other local enthusiasts to build his first aircraft, a pair of "B&W" float planes, at Lake Union. America's entry into World War I the following year kept Boeing's "Red Barn" factory on the Duwamish River busy producing Navy training planes, but peace nearly bankrupted the new company. Boeing occupied his workers building furniture and speedboats, which were popular with local bootleggers. Not coincidentally, Bill Boeing was one of their best customers.

Boeing test pilot Eddie Hubbard flew to the rescue by persuading a skeptical Boeing that the future of aviation lay in passenger and mail service. The two men flew from Vancouver, B.C., to Lake Union on March 3, 1919, to personally deliver America's first sack of international airmail — and blaze a new trail in the clouds.

Boeing's Red Barn factory

Eddie Hubbard (left) and William Boeing

Seattle voters approve purchase of Rainier Valley interurban line on March 7, 1911.

Oregon and Washington Station opens in Seattle amid fanfare on May 20, 1911, serving trains of the Union Pacific and Chicago, Milwaukee & St. Paul railroads,

First Golden Potlatch festival held in Seattle beginning July 17, 1911.

Lake Washington Ship Canal construction starts on September 1, 1911.

King County voters create Port of Seattle on September 5, 1911.

Potlatch marchers

Trolley Troubles

Most of the city's electricity was supplied by firms ultimately controlled by Stone & Webster, a national holding company based in Boston. It also ran virtually all of Seattle's streetcar lines and completed new electric interurban railroads to Tacoma and Everett during the decade. This mass transit monopoly — and its increasingly erratic service — was a fat target for municipal takeover.

In the first skirmish in 1911, city voters approved purchase of the Seattle-Renton interurban, the one line that Stone & Webster did not own. The railroad's owners balked at the last minute and the money was diverted to build a new streetcar service between downtown and Ballard in 1914.

Union maids on skates

Seattle was finally in the transit business, but the timing could not have been worse. Labor troubles, rising costs, a nickel fare fixed by law, and growing competition from private automobiles and buses had already convinced Stone & Webster to get out of the streetcar business. It negotiated a grossly inflated price for its system with Seattle Mayor Ole Hanson, and the city took over on the inauspicious date of April 1, 1918. The streetcars would run up a crippling debt before being scrapped in 1940.

Providence Hospital moves to a new Central Area building on September 24, 1911.

Denny Regrade second phase is completed on October 31, 1911.

Seattle rejects Virgil Bogue's proposed comprehensive plan on March 5, 1912, but elects progressive engineer George F. Cotterill mayor.

HMS *Titanic* hits a North Atlantic iceberg and sinks on April 14-15, 1912, taking the lives of 1,500 passengers, including six with connections to King County.

Steamship *Alameda* crashes into Colman Dock on April 25, 1912.

Rioters attack radicals during Potlatch riots on July 17 and 18, 1913.

Straightening of Duwamish River begins on October 14, 1913.

Seattle branch of the NAACP is founded on October 23, 1913.

Time Stops on Elliott Bay

At about 10:30 p.m. on April 25, 1912, the Alaska Steamship liner *Alameda* approached Colman Dock, near the foot of Madison Street. The ship's master signaled full speed astern, but the engineer below mistakenly applied full speed *ahead*. The vessel lurched forward, ramming the dock and toppling its 100-foot-tall clock tower, which in turn struck and sank the moored stern wheel steamboat *Telegraph*. Only five people were injured thanks to an alert policeman who saw the collision coming and warned passengers in the Colman Dock waiting room to run for their lives. A new tower was later erected, but then removed in the 1930s. Washington State Ferries took over Colman Dock when it acquired the Black Ball Line in 1951.

FIRE BRAND

On Tuesday February 4, 1919, two days before the Seattle General Strike started, the *Union Record* published an editorial written by the prominent Seattle School Board member Anna Louise Strong (right). She declared, "ON THURSDAY AT 10 A.M. there will be many cheering and there will be some who fear. Both of these emotions are useful, but not too much of either. We are undertaking the most tremendous move ever made by LABOR in this country, a move which will lead -- NO ONE KNOWS WHERE! We do not need hysteria. We need the iron march of labor." While 65,000 workers heeded her call, hopes for a labor-led revolution soon collapsed amid confusion, public criticism, and internal bickering.

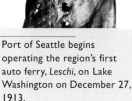

Red Scares

Labor militancy intensified during the decade. Many business conservatives, notably *Seattle Times* publisher Alden Blethen, targeted socialists and "Wobblies," as members of the Industrial Workers of the World were called. His patriotic editorials helped to incite anti-red riots during the city's 1913 Golden Potlatch festival, a precursor of Seafair.

The violence turned deadly in 1916, when a boatload of Seattle-based Wobblies exchanged gunfire with deputies and private guards while trying to dock at Everett. More deaths followed when veterans attacked the IWW's Centralia office during the first Armistice (now Veterans) Day celebration in 1919.

The famous General Strike of February 1919, however, was distinguished by its lack of violence or confrontation.

Wobblies in front of the IWW's Seattle HQ

Port of Seattle begins operating the region's first auto ferry, *Leschi*, on Lake Washington on December 27, 1913.

Nellie Cornish founds School of the Allied Arts in 1914.

Smith Tower dedication ceremony is held on July 4, 1914.

Spectacular fire destroys Grand Trunk Pacific dock and kills five on July 30, 1914.

Jefferson Park Municipal Golf Course opens on May 12, 1915.

Cedar River waters slowly inundate Moncton, beginning in the spring of 1915.

Prohibition of alcohol in Washington takes effect on midnight, December 31, 1915, and first violator is arrested at 2:55 a.m.

Ballard High School opens in January 1916.

Coliseum Theatre opens in Seattle on January 8, 1916.

Heavy snow collapses St. James Cathedral's dome on February 2, 1916.

First Boeing-built airplane, the B&W, makes its maiden flight from Lake Union on June 15, 1916.

Five Seattle Wobblies die in the "Everett Massacre" on November 5, 1916.

Seattle Metropolitans win hockey's Stanley Cup on March 26, 1917.

U. S. enters World War I on April 6, 1917.

Lake Washington Ship Canal locks are dedicated on July 4, 1917.

City Light secures a federal license on December 22, 1917, to build hydroelectric dams on the Upper Skagit River.

Frederick & Nelson opens its new store at 5th and Pine on September 3, 1918.

Cedar River's Boxley Dam bursts on December 23, 1918.

The idea for shutting down the entire city grew out of a long waterfront dispute. Socialist Seattle School Board member Anna Louise Strong lit the match with a fiery editorial in the *Union Record* (the nation's only labor daily newspaper), while most of the area's mainstream union leaders were attending a distant conference.

Sixty-five thousand workers walked off the job while unions maintained key public and health services, but the action fizzled out after a few days. Not only did the General Strike not achieve its immediate goals, it alienated the public and was exploited to justify a national crackdown on labor and leftwing groups in the tense years following the Russian Revolution of 1917.

How Dry We Were

Booze, not Bolshevism, was the cause of the decade's most radical social experiment, Prohibition. Seattle politics had long been divided between "wets" and "dries." While the latter counted many women leaders, its most forceful advocate was the Reverend Mark Matthews, who built Seattle's First Presbyterian Church into the nation's largest such congregation. Matthews also popularized the phrase "Skid Road" to describe the vice district tolerated south of Yesler Way, while he sermonized and organized against alcohol.

Nellie Cornish

Seattle and the rest of the state finally said "amen" in 1915, and the rest of the nation joined the chorus five years later. The United States also caught up in 1920 with ratification of the 19th Amendment affirming the right of women to vote. As Seattle's own history demonstrates, suffrage and Prohibition were two sides of the same coin — but the latter would prove about as popular as a Susan B. Anthony dollar.

Bonfire of bootleg booze

THE HOUSE THAT DUGDALE BUILT

Seattleites have played baseball since at least 1872, when a team named the Dolly Varden (a fish) took the field. The first professional game was played at Madison Park in 1890. Arriving in Seattle eight years later on his way to the Klondike, former pro

ballplayer Daniel Dugdale realized that there was more money in diamonds. He organized a series of regional champion teams, notably the Giants, and built Seattle its first real baseball stadium in 1913. Dugdale Park burned down in 1932, and brewer Emil Sick built his namesake stadium on the same Rainier Valley site six years later.

Daniel Dugdale with his champion Seattle Giants. Below: Dugdale Park panorama

America's first general strike paralyzes Seattle, February 6-11, 1919.

William Boeing and Eddie Hubbard deliver the first shipment of U.S. international airmail on March 3, 1919.

U.S. President Woodrow Wilson visits Seattle on September 13, 1919.

Garfield High School opens and Western Washington's first radio station starts broadcasting in 1920.

League of Women Voters holds its first national convention in Seattle following ratification of the 19th Amendment in August 1920.

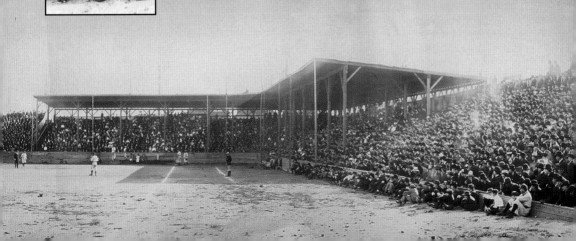

1921~1940: Boom and Gloom

Seattle's extraordinary post-fire boom finally began to cool during the 1920s. The city had grown nearly eight-fold from 42,000 in 1890 to 315,000 in 1920, and another 50,000 residents would join the fold by 1930. The balance of King County expanded from 21,000 inhabitants to 100,000 over the same period, but it remained mostly rural beyond a few close-in Seattle suburbs.

Seattle also grew denser with new neighborhoods as thousands of bungalows, cottages, and apartments sprang up to house the workers in its busy shipyards, factories, and other industries. A new downtown took shape during the 1920s with construction of major buildings such as the Bon Marche, Dexter Horton, Exchange, Skinner, and Northern Life (now Seattle) Tower.

Bird Men

As railroads had dominated the economic and civic imagination during prior decades, airplanes now captivated the public and attracted growing government attention. King County established the region's first true airfield at Sand Point in 1920, although it hoped that the Navy would quickly turn it into an air base. A skeptical and isolationist Congress delayed formal action and the County lost millions running the field.

Sand Point was the start and finish line for the first aircraft to fly around the world. Four Army Air Cruisers departed on April 6, 1924 and two of the planes returned the following September 28 after hopping 30,000 miles westward

Timeline

King County deeds Sand Point Airfield to U.S. Navy on February 1, 1921.

William Randolph Hearst buys *Seattle Post-Intelligencer* in December 1921.

First women, Bertha K. Landes and Kathryn Miracle, are elected to Seattle City Council on May 2, 1922.

Kenworth Motor Truck Corporation incorporates in Seattle in January 1923.

U.S. President Warren G. Harding dies shortly after making his final speech in Seattle on July 27, 1923.

U.S. Army flyers depart Sand Point Airfield for first aerial circumnavigation of the globe on April 6, 1924.

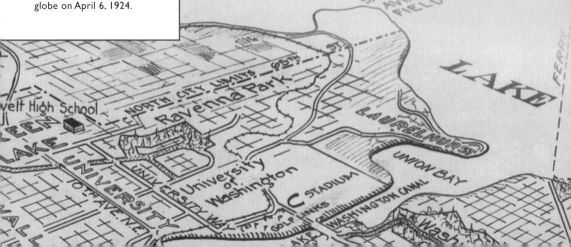

across Asia, Europe, and North America. The decade's greatest hero, Charles Lindbergh, brought the *Spirit of St. Louis* to Sand Point in 1927, the same year Congress funded construction of a naval air station.

By then Boeing had entered the airline business courtesy of a U.S. Post Office contract to transport air mail between Chicago, San Francisco, and points in-between. Boeing was recovering from its post-war doldrums with design of the fast Model 40 mail plane and relatively luxurious Model 80 tri-motor biplane — the first to employ cabin attendants later dubbed "stewardesses."

Expanding production and the impending loss of access to Sand Point's airfield led William Boeing to threaten to move his operations to Los Angeles unless a new airport was built in Seattle. With some reluctance but little choice, King County agreed to convert a former Georgetown race track and environs into Boeing Field in 1928.

Cleaning House

As the "Roaring Twenties" gained volume, Prohibition was enforced with declining enthusiasm in King County. Deputies and federal agents made headlines smashing rural stills and leading high-profile raids against the posh Rainier Club and famous tipplers such as Bill Boeing, but their efforts did little to slow the river of hooch gushing southward from Canada via land and sea.

Charles Lindbergh at Sand Point

OLYMPIC METTLE

On December 6, 1924, the posh Olympic Hotel opened at 5th Avenue and University Street, on the original site of the Territorial University. Two thousand members of Seattle's social elite attended the grand opening celebration. The hotel's construction was financed by a successful community bond sale which enlisted the support of thousands of citizens. Restored in 1981 and now managed by the international Four Seasons group, the Olympic still reigns as one of America's premier hotels.

Federal law grants U.S. citizenship to all American Indians on June 2, 1924.

Ku Klux Klan rally attracts 13,000 in Issaquah on July 26, 1924.

Hydroelectric power from Skagit River reaches Seattle on September 14, 1924.

Olympic Hotel opens for business on December 6, 1924.

Montlake Bridge is completed in June 1925.

Seattle elects its first woman mayor, Bertha K. Landes, on March 9, 1926.

Boeing enters airline business by winning federal air mail contract for Chicago-San Francisco route on January 28, 1927.

Mary Davenport-Engberg led the Seattle Symphony in 1921 as the first woman conductor of a major U.S. orchestra

52

OLYMPIC MEDALS

At the age of just 19, Seattle swimmer Helene Madison (pictured here with Buster Crabbe) dazzled the athletic world by winning three Gold Medals during the 1932 Olympic Games in Los Angeles. Expectations were high for more achievements at the 1936 games in Berlin, but Madison was disqualified due to some minor "professional" appearances. Meanwhile, the University of Washington's rowing team returned from Nazi Germany with its own Gold Medal. After failed attempts to attract Hollywood's attention, Madison died in Seattle and obscurity in 1970.

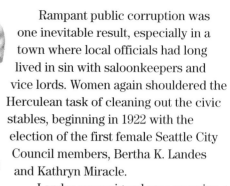

Sound motion pictures debut in Seattle at the Blue Mouse on March 18, 1927.

Lindbergh lands the *Spirit of St. Louis* in Seattle on September 13, 1927.

Jewish Federation of Greater Seattle is created in January 1928.

3rd Avenue, ca. 1940

Rampant public corruption was one inevitable result, especially in a town where local officials had long lived in sin with saloonkeepers and vice lords. Women again shouldered the Herculean task of cleaning out the civic stables, beginning in 1922 with the election of the first female Seattle City Council members, Bertha K. Landes and Kathryn Miracle.

Landes campaigned on a promise of "municipal housekeeping" in 1926 and defeated Mayor Edward "Doc" Brown, a flamboyant dentist, to become the first female chief executive of a major American city. Her broom was powerless, however, against the mounting debts of the city's streetcar system, an otherwise efficient service whose finances were crushed under the weight of its original purchase price and hobbled by state restrictions on non-fare box subsidies. Frank Edwards offered a "secret plan" to bail out the system and unseated Landes after one term in 1928.

The Wheels Come Off

None of this was accidental: The street railway's original owner, Stone & Webster, skillfully manipulated the ongoing crisis in a bid to take over its chief rival, Seattle City Light. It overplayed its hand when Edwards fired City Light chief J.D. Ross in 1931. Voters promptly recalled the mayor, and his successor rehired Ross — but the streetcars continued to drown in red ink chiefly because of competition from automobiles.

Since World War I, cars had multiplied like rabbits and government began to respond with

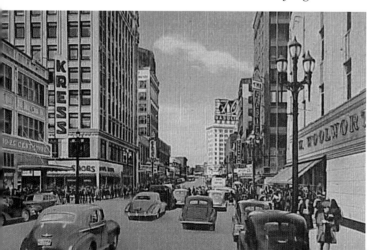

longer and better roads. Highway 99 created a paved route from Canada to Oregon, paralleling the route of the electric interurban railways that had previously linked Puget Sound cities. Rail service between Seattle and Tacoma was the first to end, in 1928, and the Seattle-Everett line shut down a decade later.

Seattle commuters remained loyal to their aging but reliable streetcars, rejecting a plan to replace them with buses and newfangled "trackless trolleys" in 1937. Three years later, city officials reluctantly faced the inevitable, and accepted a federal loan to scrap the streetcars in 1940. That same year, the state proudly dedicated its new Lake Washington Floating Bridge, lighting a slow fuse for the suburban explosion to come.

Civic Auditorium, now the Opera House, ca. 1928

Hard Landing

The New York Stock Exchange crash of October 1929 was but one avalanche as the world slid into a deep economic crevasse. Between 1929 and 1932, the cargo crossing Port of Seattle docks dropped by three fourths, downtown and residential construction screeched to a halt, banks collapsed, and thousands of workers transferred from assembly lines to soup lines.

HER HONOR THE MAYOR

On March 9, 1926, Bertha Knight Landes was elected mayor of Seattle and became the first woman executive of a major American city. She followed through on her pledge to perform "municipal housekeeping" and led an honest, scandal-free administration — a rarity in Seattle history up to that time. Unfortunately, she could not balance the books of the city's bankrupt streetcar system, and voters replaced her after a single two-year term with Frank Edwards in 1928. He in turn was recalled three years later after firing popular City Light Superintendent J.D. Ross. Landes remained active in local and national civic affairs and women's organizations until her death in 1943.

Don Ibsen invents waterskis on Lake Washington in 1928.

Boeing Field, Seattle's first municipal airport, opens on July 26, 1928.

Interurban train service between Seattle and Tacoma ends on December 30, 1928.

Stock market crashes on "Black Tuesday," October 29, 1929.

City Light dedicates Skagit River's Diablo Dam on August 27, 1930.

Final Denny Regrade is completed on December 10, 1930.

Japanese American Citizens League (JACL) founded in Seattle in 1930.

Seattle population grows to 365,000 during 1920s and King County tops 460,000.

Seattle voters recall Mayor Frank Edwards on July 13, 1931, after he fires City Light head J.D. Ross (who is promptly reappointed by the new mayor, Robert Harlin).

St. Mark's Episcopal Cathedral is dedicated on April 25, 1931.

BUDDY, CAN YOU SPARE A NAIL?

In October 1931, an unemployed lumberjack by the name of Jesse Jackson and 20 others started building shacks on nine acres of vacant shipyards owned by the Port of Seattle a few blocks south of Pioneer Square. They assembled 50 shanties in a few days and named their settlement "Hooverville." After trying to burn out the squatters, the city relented and allowed them to stay on the condition that they adhere to safety and sanitary rules. A census taken during March 1934 counted 632 men and seven women living in 479 shanties. Their ages ranged from 15 to 73. Included were 292 foreign born Caucasians, 186 Caucasians born in the United States, 120 Filipinos, 29 African Americans, three Costa Ricans, two Mexicans, two Indians, two Eskimos, and one Chilean. Hooverville burned down in April 1941, by which time local defense industries were hiring again in anticipation of another world war.

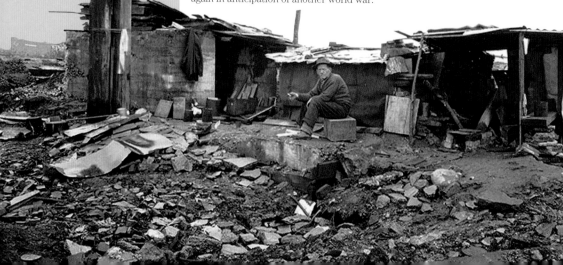

In late 1931, hundreds of unemployed men (and a few women) established a shantytown in an idle shipyard south of Pioneer Square. They mockingly called it Hooverville after President Herbert Hoover, who himself became unemployed with the elections of 1932.

Franklin Delano Roosevelt's landslide victory supplied fresh hope but not instant recovery, although the repeal of Prohibition provided temporary relief in 1933. The New Deal re-energized labor and leftwing organizers who had been sidelined since the General Strike of 1919. They were quick to act, assembling powerful coalitions such as the Washington Commonwealth Federation in 1934, and leading dramatic strikes.

Harry Bridges in London

Longshoremen and maritime workers strike West Coast and Seattle on May 9, 1934.

Federal trust-busters force Boeing conglomerate United Aircraft & Transport to break up on September 26, 1934.

Liberal-left Washington Commonwealth Federation is founded on June 8, 1935.

Ferry *Kalakala* starts daily service between Seattle and Bremerton on July 3, 1935.

Dave Beck

Happy Days?

One of the most violent labor confrontations idled docks from Bellingham to San Diego and pitted leftist Harry Bridges' militant Longshoremen against Seattle-born Dave Beck's more business-friendly Teamsters. Bridges won the bloody 1934 battle, but Beck was also established as a national force in labor. Two years later, *Seattle Post-Intelligencer* workers challenged and defeated William Randolph Hearst, the nation's most powerful publisher, in

FLYING BOAT

During the 1930s, transoceanic travel was beyond the capability of all but a handful of aircraft. The solution was offered by giant dirigibles and ever larger "flying boats" — multi-engine airplanes with boat-like hulls. The most luxurious and successful of these was Boeing's Model 314 "Clipper," which first flew in 1938 and opened the Atlantic Ocean to scheduled airline service in 1939, filling a void left by the spectacular explosion of the *Hindenburg* two years earlier. A dozen Clippers were built and operated through World War II. Made obsolete by new and faster airliners, the last Clipper was scrapped in 1951.

FLYING BIRD

Between 1935 and 1967, the most distinctive vessel on Puget Sound was the ferry *Kalakala*. The ship's gleaming streamlined superstructure epitomized 1930s modernity, but it actually rested on the burned-out hull of the *Peralta*, an older and star-crossed San Francisco ferry. Refitted and launched anew at Kirkland in 1935, the *Kalakala* (a name meaning "flying bird" in Chinook jargon) was operated by the Black Ball Line and then the State of Washington until 1967. The vessel was later towed to Alaska and beached for use as a cannery. Volunteers led by sculptor Peter Bevis rescued it in 1998 and returned it to Seattle, where it is undergoing renovation.

Floating Bridge

Upon completion in June 1940, the Lacey V. Murrow Floating Bridge was the largest floating object in the world. Named for the State Secretary of Transportation (and brother of broadcaster Edward R. Murrow), the bridge spanned Lake Washington between Seattle's Mount Baker ridge and Mercer Island as part of U.S. Highway 10, later Interstate 90. State plans to expand I-90 triggered years of law suits and political protests during the 1970s. Following construction of a parallel span, the original sank while under repair in a storm on November 25, 1990.

Boeing Flying Fortress B-17 prototype takes her maiden flight on July 28, 1935.

Eddie Bauer invents the down parka in Seattle in 1936.

Seattle Congressman Marion Zioncheck commits suicide on August 8, 1936, and is succeeded by Warren G. Magnuson.

Rowing crew of the University of Washington wins the Olympic Gold Medal on August 14, 1936.

Newspaper Guild strikes *Seattle Post-Intelligencer* on August 19, 1936.

Seattle voters reject plan to scrap municipal streetcars on March 9, 1937.

First Boeing Clipper lifts off from Elliott Bay on June 7, 1938.

Pioneer Square Totem is damaged by arsonist on October 22, 1938, and replaced two years later.

REI (Recreational Equipment Inc.) cooperative is founded in Seattle in 1939.

Interurban rail service between Everett and Seattle ends February 20, 1939.

Nazi Germany invades Poland on September 1, 1939, triggering World War II in Europe.

Federal government approves loan to build Yesler Terrace public housing project on December 2, 1939.

another bitter strike. Both actions contributed to passage of new federal laws finally recognizing the right of workers to bargain collectively.

William Boeing was not whistling "Happy days are here again" as anti-trust Democrats targeted his giant United Aircraft and Transport conglomerate, which included United Air Lines and numerous other companies. The combine was broken up in 1934 amid a disastrous reorganization of the nation's air mail system, and Boeing bid a bitter farewell to the industry he had helped to create.

The Boeing Company barely survived but it regained its technological edge with a succession of revolutionary aircraft starting with its 1933 design for the first true airliner, the Model 247. It was followed by elegant Pan Am Clipper flying boat, and the sleek four-engine Stratoliner, the world's first pressurized airliner.

The most important airplane to roll out of Boeing's Plant 2 hangars was the B-17. On its maiden flight in 1935, an awestruck *Seattle Times* reporter gushed that it looked like a "flying fortress." Unfortunately, isolationists still controlled military purse strings, and there was little money to buy the powerful four-engine bomber, on whose design the company had literally bet the Red Barn.

World war would prove to be Boeing's — and Seattle's — true savior.

Alice Brougham with columnist and onetime Rainier Emmett Watson

THE VIEW FROM TIGHTWAD HILL

In 1937, brewer Emil Sick bought Seattle's Pacific Coast League franchise, the Indians, and renamed the team the Rainiers after his most popular beverage. The following year, he built his namesake stadium on the former site of Dugdale Park. Penurious fans could watch games for free from nearby "Tightwad Hill" as the Rainiers dominated the PCL for nearly three decades thanks to star players such as Fred Hutchinson (Number 29 below).

Both Sick and Hutchinson died in 1964, and the latter's brother William later founded the Fred Hutchinson Cancer Research Center in his memory. Meanwhile, Seattle wooed the American League, but its first franchise, the Pilots, played one disappointing season at Sicks' in 1969 before bolting for Milwaukee. The Mariners debuted in King County's new domed stadium in 1977, and Sicks' Stadium was demolished two years later. The Kingdome met the same fate in 2000, after the Mariners relocated to Safeco Field.

Lake Washington Floating Bridge is dedicated on July 2, 1940.

First peacetime draft takes effect on October 16, 1940.

Seattle Mayor Arthur Langlie is elected governor on November 5, 1940.

Population of Seattle stagnates at 368,000 during 1930s while all of King County grows modestly to 500,000 residents.

Hooverville burns down on April 10, 1941.

Trackless trolleys and buses replace streetcars in Seattle Transit System on April 13, 1941.

War declared against Japan on December 8, 1941.

Installation of anti-aircraft guns force children from city parks in January 1942.

Boeing hires Florise Spearman, first African American employee, in January 1942.

FDR signs Executive Order 9066, mandating internment of West Coast Japanese Americans, on February 19, 1942.

Port of Seattle agrees to build new regional airport on March 7, 1942.

Japanese Americans are ordered to evacuate Seattle on April 21, 1942.

Seattle Symphony conductor Sir Thomas Beecham warns that Seattle is becoming a "cultural dustbin" in April 1942.

1941~1960:
Hot and Cold Wars

Fearing a second world war, the United States began to build up its armed forces in the late 1930s, which helped to revitalize the Depression-becalmed economy of greater Seattle. Following the December 7, 1941, attack on Pearl Harbor, the region's aircraft and ship builders shifted into high gear. Every sector of business and domestic life was affected by the war effort. The society underwent dramatic change as women took the place of men on production lines, thousands of Japanese Americans were interned, and equal numbers of African Americans migrated to the Northwest in search of defense jobs.

In October 1940, the first peacetime draft took effect. Boeing began turning out B-17s for the Royal Air Force under the Lend-Lease program by which the U.S. aided Britain while remaining officially neutral. Civil Defense committees were established and conducted drills and practiced blackouts.

Meanwhile, city workers ripped up Seattle's street railways and melted down the old streetcars. Some of the scrap was reportedly sold to Japan before its relations with the U.S. began to sour mid-1941. By then, few believed that the United States could avoid entanglement in the spreading world conflict, but nothing prepared the community for the shock of December 7, 1941.

Young men head for Seattle's enlistment center

Collateral Damage

Seattle's Japan Town, then the West Coast's second largest, immediately found itself torn between new loyalties and old prejudices. The FBI arrested several Japanese-born Seattle residents on December 7, and their neighbors found themselves under suspicion despite the Japanese American community's obvious and deep patriotism.

Local community and religious leaders urged patience and tolerance, but as news from the Pacific Theater went from bad to worse, the national public mood turned uglier, especially in California. On February 19, 1942, President Roosevelt signed Executive Order 9066 directing the internment of all aliens and citizens of Japanese descent on the West Coast.

A few brave white and Japanese American citizens protested this mass violation of Constitutional rights, but the internment proceeded. After only a few days' warning, King County's 9,700 Japanese Americans were forcibly "evacuated" to the Puyallup Fair Grounds (ironically dubbed "Camp Harmony") and then shipped to camps such as Minidoka, Idaho, for the duration of the war.

THE LAST STREETCAR

On April 13, 1941, the Seattle Municipal Railway's last streetcar completed its final run along 8th Avenue NW in Ballard. The old routes were taken over by buses and electric "trackless trolleys" purchased with a $10.2 million federal loan. Streetcars would not be seen again in Seattle until 1982, when downtown's Waterfront Streetcar entered service. Above: 4th Avenue stripped of its tracks

Arsenal of Democracy

Orders for aircraft, ships, and other war materiel poured into Puget Sound and the entire state, lifting its moribund economy. In January 1943, Washington Secretary of State Belle Reeves wrote, "No state has been more profoundly affected economically by the expansion of war industries than Washington." Seattle ranked as one of the top three cities in the nation in war contracts per capita, and Washington state ranked as one of the top

WAR EXTRA

WAR DECLARED!
U. S. FLEET SAILS!
BATTLESHIP BOMBED
2ND RAID ON HONOLULU!
The Seattle Daily Times 3¢ SUNDAY EXTRA!

RALLY 'ROUND THE FLAG

Thousands of citizens filled University Street in front of the Olympic Hotel on May 2, 1942, to dedicate Victory Square as a civic focal point for Seattle's World War II home front. The plaza featured wooden representations of Thomas Jefferson's Monticello home and the Washington Monument, which was inscribed with a growing list of local war dead. Hollywood stars such as Lana Turner and Bob Hope performed there during frequent War Bond drives.

A DATE THAT WILL LIVE IN INFAMY

Waitress Irene Wilson had just arrived for her shift at downtown Seattle's popular Igloo Restaurant on Sunday morning, December 7, 1941, when a customer entered with a newspaper. It was a moment Irene recalled vividly almost 50 years later. "He had the paper folded over, you know, so that you could just make out the headlines. He held the paper up so that everyone in the restaurant could see. The headline was just three letters — WAR. The whole place was dead silent. Like we couldn't hardly move. Then over the [counter radios] they made the announcement 'all men report...' and the men just got up at once. The women, we were left there, dumb on our seats with blank faces. Nobody paid for anything, they just got up. They didn't even wait for their orders. Men just left the line. I couldn't believe it. I thought that was the end. That we were all going to die."

COURAGE OF HIS CONVICTIONS

On May 16, 1942, Gordon Hirabayashi, a University of Washington senior, Quaker, and conscientious objector, drove with his attorney to the Seattle FBI office and challenged the Army's internment of all Japanese Americans and their immigrant elders on the West Coast. To comply, he wrote, "I would be giving helpless consent to the denial of practically all of the things which give me incentive to live." He was promptly convicted of violating exclusion and curfew laws, and federal judges, including famed liberal Supreme Court Justice William O. Douglas, rejected his appeal. The justice system reconsidered in 1986 and 1987, and paved the way for national reparations for all Japanese American internees.

two states. Airplane and ship contracts in 1943-1944 were valued at three times the total of all manufacturing in the state in 1939. Boeing's payroll, which numbered about 7,500 persons in 1940, listed more than 32,000 workers in Seattle and Renton by 1944.

To maintain production, local industries turned to African American workers, previously locked out of the skilled labor pool. The influx quadrupled Seattle's black population to nearly 16,000, but 70 percent found themselves confined to just 10 Central Area census tracts, including much of the former Japan Town, by dint of restrictive covenants and other forms of de facto segregation.

Thousands of women also joined the war effort on previously all-male assembly lines, and helped to establish the archetype of "Rosie the Riveter." Both the racial and the sexual integration of the workforce were intended to be temporary, but planted seeds for a permanent social revolution.

Flying and Floating Fortresses

Swarms of new B-17 Flying Fortresses lifted off from Boeing Field, and production would total 6,981 by war's end. Bombing operations in the Pacific required a longer range airplane and Boeing went to work on the top secret B-29. Few knew that a deadly airplane crash into South Seattle's Frye Meat Packing Plant on February 18, 1943,

Victory Square dedicated in Seattle on May 2, 1942.

Holly Park housing project opens on August 1, 1942.

Prototype Boeing B-29 crashes into Seattle's Frye Packing Plant on February 18, 1943.

Boeing Company begins recruiting women workers from across the country in June 1943.

Colman Swimming Pool is integrated in 1944.

Black soldiers riot at Fort Lawton on August 14, 1944.

Seattle Congressman Warren G. Magnuson wins election to the U.S. Senate on November 7, 1944.

Left-liberal Washington Commonwealth Federation disbands on March 18, 1945.

President Truman announces V-E Day, Victory-in-Europe, on May 8, 1945.

An atomic bomb is dropped on Hiroshima on August 6, 1945.

World War II ends on August 14, 1945. The final count of Washington state citizens who died in combat or direct military service will top 6,250.

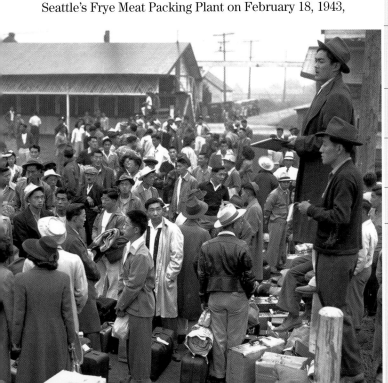

Left: Japanese American internees at "Camp Harmony"

involved one of the first two prototypes of the new Stratofortress, with famed test pilot Eddie Allen at the controls.

Boeing Field, Renton's Bryn Mar Airport, and Tacoma's McChord Field were all inducted for airplane production and military operations, prompting the federal government to seek development of a new airport for the region. When the state and local governments declined, the Port of Seattle shouldered the task to create today's Seattle-Tacoma International Airport, which first opened to military traffic in 1944.

Puget Sound-area shipyards constructed an unbelievable number of war vessels. At the peak of the war, 55,000 men and women turned out scores of warships and support vessels at the combined Todd Shipyards/Seattle-Tacoma Shipbuilding. Yet more toiled day and night at Puget Sound Bridge and Drydock/Associated Shipbuilders to launch scores of minesweepers and other vessels.

The Suburbs Do Their Part

State forests supplied billions of board-feet to build everything from barracks to minesweepers (steel being a trigger for magnetic mines). Specialized lumber products such as water-resistant plywood were developed as substitutes for critically scarce metals.

The Japanese American internment cost the region some of its most productive farmers, but others -- notably Italian Americans -- took over the fields to supply the military and home front while

B-29 "BOMBS" SEATTLE

On February 18, 1943, the second of Boeing's top-secret XB-29 prototype "Superfortress" bombers caught fire 20 minutes after takeoff from Boeing Field and crashed into South Seattle's Frye Packing Plant while struggling to land. Lead Boeing test pilot Eddie Allen and 10 crewmen perished

along with 19 workers in the meat processing factory. While the event could not be concealed, the identity of the aircraft — two of whose successors would drop the first atomic bombs on Japan — remained classified until the end of World War II.

Women pilots "ferried" Boeing bombers to the front

local citizens cultivated "Victory Gardens" to help feed themselves. Local fishermen delivered virtually all of the salmon canned in Washington and Alaska to the Army and Navy.

The Puget Sound Naval Shipyard in Bremerton commissioned 19 major ships, including destroyers and escort aircraft carriers, and repaired many battle-damaged ships. Kirkland's Lake Washington Shipyard employed another 6,000 workers to repair dozens of merchant vessels and ferries during the war and to turn out ships for the Navy.

Renton gained a huge Boeing airplane factory early in the war that turned out hundreds of B-29 Superfortresses. The Pacific Car and Foundry plant there produced thousands of tanks and military vehicles during the war.

In Bellevue, which didn't incorporate as a city until 1953, the Coast Guard appropriated the old whaling dock on Meydenbauer Bay and converted the whaling vessels for military duty. As war workers rented whatever shelter they could find on the Eastside, Overlake Transit scheduled 26 bus trips a day to carry commuters across the new Floating Bridge. Despite war rationing, the government permitted construction of the first few buildings in what became Bellevue Shopping Square on former strawberry fields once tended by Japanese American families.

Warren G. Magnuson

It's Finally Over Over There

At 4 p.m. Pacific Time on August 14, 1945, President Harry Truman announced Japan's surrender on national radio. Thousands of jubilant civilians and servicemen and women poured into downtown Seattle's streets. Among them, a young sailor named Ole Scarpelli climbed a street lamp and flashed the "V" sign at some admiring secretaries — not knowing that the moment would be immortalized by a *Seattle Post Intelligencer* photographer.

Ending with a Bang

After the war ended in Europe on May 8, 1945, all efforts turned to a planned invasion of the Japanese home islands. This operation was averted on August 6, 1945, when a B-29 Superfortress (built in Wichita, by the way) dropped an atomic bomb on Hiroshima. Japan surrendered after a second bomb destroyed Nagasaki.

Washington residents finally learned what had been going on at Hanford in Eastern Washington, where plutonium had been prepared there for use in the bomb under the tightest possible security. Thus, Washington had both designed the plane and refined the nuclear fuel that ended a World War and ushered in the Atomic Age.

The state mourned the loss of more than 6,250 of its sons and daughters, defense workers were soon laid off by the thousands, and women traded in rivet guns for baby bottles. Any dreams of returning to "normalcy" would soon be dashed,

Seattle's Jackson Street Community Council, Jewish Community Center, Civil Rights Congress, and Bellevue's Pacific Northwest Arts Fair are all founded in 1946.

Seattle adopts its first new City Charter in half a century on March 12, 1946.

Watch the Skies!

While flying alone near Mt. Rainier on June 24, 1947, Boise businessman Kenneth Arnold observed nine shiny objects "flying like a saucer would if you skipped it across the water." Soon, other people were spotting "flying saucers," and the *Seattle Post-Intelligencer* published the first photograph of a "mystery disc," snapped by a Lake City man on July 4 (it turned out to be a weather balloon). The phenomenon spread across the nation when the Army reported (and then retracted) that a saucer had crashed near Roswell, New Mexico. Not to be outdone, two Tacoma log salvagers claimed that they had seen a giant "flying doughnut" explode over Maury Island and had the bits to prove it. Although a crude hoax, their accounts of a visit by a menacing "man in black" and subsequent government cover-up were permanently implanted in the public imagination.

for the war had changed the region's economy, population, and social structure in profound and permanent ways.

Cold War

Jubilation over the end of World War II was brief as the realities of a brave new post-war world began to sink in. Once busy shipyards, docks, and airplane factories ratcheted down defense-related production, laying off thousands of workers as the nation sank into a recession.

Ivar Haglund with his, "Acres of Clams" and popular diver's mask for kids

The local economy eventually recovered along with that of the nation, and by the late 1940s a new "Cold War" dominated headlines. Greater Seattle benefited to the degree that Boeing became a major supplier of the jet bombers and nuclear missiles that provided deterence through "mutual assured destruction," but residents also suffered the anxieties and paranoia that came to characterize the 1950s.

More subtle forces also worked below the surface to transform the metropolitan community. Seattle took the first tentative steps to acknowledge its thousands of new African American citizens and other minorities. Schools struggled to cope with surging Baby Boom enrollments, and burgeoning suburbs began to shift the epicenter of population growth away from the central city and erode its former political monopoly.

In contrast to the cozy domestic tranquility projected by the era's television situation comedies, seismic tensions built up during the 1950s which would shake the community's foundations in the next decade.

Un-American Activities

In the first heady days following the war's end, progressives watched reforms in postwar Europe and hoped to tap the new sense of national unity to advance a few changes of their own, especially some form of national health insurance. Local unions, granges, and consumer advocates incorporated

---

Ivar Haglund opens Ivar's Acres of Clams at Pier 54 on July 22, 1946.

University of Washington opens a medical school on October 2, 1946.

Group Health Cooperative begins offering medical care and hospital services on January 1, 1947.

Dorothy Stimson Bullitt purchases future KING radio in 1947.

Un-American Activities bill passes the Washington State Legislature on March 8, 1947.

Kenneth Arnold reports seeing the world's first "flying saucers" near Mt. Rainier on June 24, 1947.

Scheduled airline service from Seattle to the Far East begins on July 15, 1947.

The *Seattle Star* ends publication on August 13, 1947.

66

Protesters at Seattle's Canwell hearings

Seattle public school system hires its first black instructors, Thelma Dewitty and Marita Johnson, in September 1947.

Boeing's first jet bomber, the XB-47, makes its maiden flight on December 17, 1947.

Aeronautical Machinists Union begins five-month strike against Boeing on April 22, 1948.

Fr. Albert Lemieux announces new Seattle University charter on May 28, 1948.

First wide-audience TV broadcast is seen around Puget Sound on November 25, 1948.

Washington State Legislature enacts Fair Employment Practices Act (FEPA) in 1949.

University of Washington fires three faculty members for leftwing politics on January 22, 1949.

Severe 7.1 magnitude earthquake hits Puget Sound area, killing eight and damaging numerous buildings, on April 13, 1949.

Group Health Cooperative in late 1945, now one of the nation's leading consumer-owned health care systems. It was condemned as "socialized medicine" by state and local medical associations, which also opposed the University of Washington's creation of a medical school in 1948.

Local reform entered a long winter as relations between the United States and the Soviet Union chilled and both sides settled in for the Cold War. Fear of Communist subversion caused the State Legislature to authorize a joint committee to ferret out "Un-American" activities in 1947, long before Wisconsin Senator Joe McCarthy would lend his name to the cause. The Committee's chairman, Albert Canwell, soon focused on Seattle as a hotbed of unwholesome ideas.

Red hunts intensified with Mao Zedong's 1949 victory in China and the onset of the Korean conflict a year later. The University of Washington fired three professors for leftist leanings, unions expelled radicals and militants, and Communists such as newspaperman Terry Pettus were prosecuted. Famed Filipino writer Carlos Bulosan was blacklisted and died in poverty, state pension reformer Bill Pennock committed suicide, and Florence and Burton James lost their Seattle Repertory Theater (now the Glenn Hughes Playhouse in the University District). Half a century later, the UW apologized for its collaboration in these purges.

Minorities eked out some gains locally. Recognizing the dramatic growth of Seattle's African American population during World War II,

Rockets help send a B-47 airborne

Mystical Markings

In 1953, *Life Magazine* profiled four Seattle area painters: Mark Tobey, Morris Graves, Guy Anderson, and Kenneth Callahan. Although their individual styles were quite distinct, *Life* framed them in a group portrait of "Mystic Painters of the Northwest." The four men were friends and occasional collaborators, and in turn served as mentors and teachers to several generations of regional artists in many fields. By dint of age, bearing, and early critical success, Tobey became the acknowledged dean of the greater Seattle painting scene in the mid-20th century. Born in 1890 in Illinois and trained in Chicago and New York, he arrived in Seattle in 1923 to teach and paint. Urban life, and especially the Pike Place Market's motley multitudes, were among his favorite subjects. Influenced by travels to Europe and Japan and encounters with Baha'i and Zen, Tobey developed a calligraphic "white writing" style infused with a profound spirituality and sympathetic humanity. He left Seattle in 1960 to make his home in Basel, Switzerland, but returned for a triumphant visit in 1971 five years before his death.

Mark Tobey, 1971 (Art Hupy)

the School District hired its first black instructors in 1947 and the state banned racial discrimination in the work place in 1949. Seattle elected its first black State Representative, Republican Carl Stokes, the following year, but racial tensions would simmer throughout the decade with now familiar complaints of police brutality, segregated schools, and job discrimination.

Boeing Falls and Rises

Following World War II, the federal government encouraged the consolidation of the nation's aircraft industry. Boeing was one of the lucky survivors, having proved its engineering skills and production abilities by turning out thousands of B-17 and B-29 bombers. The latter provided the basic design for an improved B-50, the C-97 transport, and the KC-97 aerial tanker.

As early as 1943, Boeing was working on an aviation revolution: multi-jet bombers that could race to their targets at near the speed of sound with atomic bombs. The first of these, the XB-47, lifted off from Boeing Field on December 17, 1947. Boeing's second strategic bomber, the giant B-52, would follow in April 1952 — and it remains on active duty in the nation's Air Force a half-century later.

Seattle-Tacoma International Airport dedicates modern terminal on July 9, 1949.

City Light's Ross Dam is completed on August 18, 1949.

Central Seattle elects Republican Carl Stokes as King County's first black State Representative (and Washington's second black legislator) in 1950.

Northgate Shopping Mall opens on April 21, 1950.

Korean War begins on June 25, 1950.

Hydroplane *Slo-Mo-Shun IV* establishes world speed record on June 26, 1950.

Seafair is held for the first time in King County on August 11-20, 1950.

The ferry *Leschi* makes its last run, ending ferry service on Lake Washington on August 31, 1950.

These military orders were not enough, however, to sustain Boeing's huge wartime payroll or to meet worker demands for long-postponed raises. Machinists struck in 1948, and Boeing turned to an unlikely ally, Dave Beck's Teamsters, to help break the union. The gambit did not work, but the machinists returned to work after five months with little to show for the stoppage.

Civilian air travel returned to normal and began to expand. Boeing adapted its design for the C-97 to produce its first postwar airliner, the luxurious double-decked 377 Stratocruiser, in 1947. Northwest Airlines, which would become one of Boeing's major customers, opened Seattle's first scheduled routes to Tokyo, Shanghai, and Manila that year. Its passengers at Seattle-Tacoma International Airport would have to wait in prefab buildings until 1949, when the Port of Seattle planners dedicated a new terminal, hailed as the state of the art.

Ironically, Boeing would soon make the terminal obsolete. Company engineers modified early plans for the KC-135 aerial tanker to produce a radical new jetliner. The Dash-80 prototype of the 707 took to the air for the first time on July 15, 1954, and test pilot "Tex" Johston stunned Seafair crowds a year later by putting the plane through dramatic aileron rolls. The plane could not land at Sea-Tac until the runway was lengthened in 1958.

Seattle voters approve City Light purchase of Puget Power assets within city limits on November 7, 1950.

Population of Seattle tops 465,000 and that of King County exceeds 730,000 in 1950.

Washington State Ferries begins operations on June 1, 1951.

Seattle begins year-long celebration of its centennial on November 13, 1951, and Murray Morgan publishes *Skid Road.*

UP AND OVER

On August 7, 1955, Alvin M. "Tex" Johnston stunned the crowd at the Seafair Gold Cup hydroplane race on Lake Washington by putting the prototype Dash-80, the precursor to the Boeing 707, though a complete aileron roll. Flying at more than 400 miles per hour just 400 feet above the water, Johnston commenced a sudden ascent. The jet's swept-back wings spiraled as the 128-foot-long, 160,000 pound plane rolled, flying for a short time upside down. Then, for extra measure, Johnston performed a second roll — all a complete surprise to Boeing President Allen who watched the fly-over with a group of airline executives. Allen asked a guest with a heart problem if he could borrow his pills, but the potential 707 customers were duly impressed.

All Shook Up

As people watched ever larger and faster aircraft race across the sky, they sometimes saw unexpected things. One June 24, 1947, a lone pilot named Kenneth Arnold noticed a line of shiny objects skipping along the Cascades near Mt. Rainier. Within days, reports of "flying saucers" and "mystery disks" made headlines across the region and then the nation.

HARDLY SLOW MOTION

On June 26, 1950, the hydroplane *Slo-Mo-Shun IV*, piloted by Stan Sayres, shattered the world speed record on water. His speed of 160.3235 mph across the waves of Lake Washington bettered the previous record of 141 mph set in 1939 in England. The run was completed about 7:10 a.m., so early that few people witnessed the event, but tens of thousands watched Sayres dominate that year's Gold Cup Races in the Detroit River. The Seattle-built *Slo-Mo-Shun* and her descendents transformed the sport of boat racing and established Seattle as its new capital in time for the first Seafair festivals.

Back on earth, a temblor measuring 7.1 on the Richter Scale shook all of Puget Sound on April 13, 1949, toppling older buildings and killing eight. But postwar technology, not tectonics, would do far more to shake and transform local society, and none more so than television.

TV made its local debut on Thanksgiving Day 1948. Only 1,000 homes could tune in KSRC's flickering images of a high school football game between West Seattle and Wenatchee, but KING radio's new owner, Dorothy Bullitt, instantly recognized the medium's potential and bought the TV station.

Early programming included coverage of Seattle's new Seafair festival, first organized in 1950 to help celebrate the centennial of the city's founding. The highlights of these events were the hydroplane races, which had been revolutionized in 1950 when Stan Sayres' locally built *Slo-Mo-Shun IV* hydroplane topped 160 miles per hour on Lake Washington.

Along with "Top-40" AM radio stations such as KJR and KOL, television also exposed Seattle to the revolution sweeping popular music. Ed Sullivan may have blacked out Elvis Presley's swiveling hips on his national TV show, but thousands of Seattle teenagers jammed Sicks' Stadium to see the real thing on September 1, 1957.

1949 earthquake damage in Pioneer Square

Frye Art Museum opens on Seattle's First Hill in 1952.

Paul Robeson overcomes censors to perform at the Civic Auditorium on May 20, 1952.

Boeing B-52 Stratofortress prototype takes its first flight on April 15, 1952.

King County voters reject new "home rule" charter on November 5, 1952.

City of Bellevue incorporates on March 31, 1953.

Alaskan Way Viaduct is completed along Seattle waterfront on April 4, 1953.

Early Seafair queen and her escorts

70

Strikers close *The Seattle Times* for 94 days beginning on July 16, 1953.

Seattle annexes Lake City and extends city limits north to 145th Street in January 1954.

Dick's Drive-in begins serving hamburgers in Seattle on January 28, 1954.

Dash-80 prototype of the Boeing 707 first flies on July 15, 1954.

Allied Arts of Seattle is formed on October 3, 1954.

SEATTLE'S VANISHING AUTO-TECTURE

Seattle has long boasted of quirky roadside buildings designed to attract passing drivers. Alas, Green Lake's Twin Teepees Restaurant and downtown's twin-domed Igloo Cafe are now gone, but one still barely survives: the Hat 'n' Boots gas station near Georgetown. Its unique cowboy-hat-shaped office and giant cowboy boots housing restrooms first opened in 1955, and earned a U.S. Patent the following year. Although abandoned since the 1970s, the local community hopes to relocate and restore it as part of a new Georgetown park.

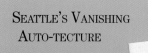

The Shape of Things to Come

In 1956, President Eisenhower launched construction of a "national defense" interstate highway system — including the future I-5 and I-90. The automobile had already become the primary determinant of metropolitan growth, allowing families to build homes farther and farther away from Seattle's factories and offices.

Between 1950 and 1960, King County's suburbs added 110,000 new residents. As the Lake Washington Floating Bridge filled with Eastside commuters, the ferry *Leschi* completed her last cross-lake run in 1950, and one of the nation's first shopping centers, Northgate, opened to serve north end communities. The following year, Washington State took over the region's private Black Ball ferry system, and began drawing up plans for highways and bridges to unite Puget Sound in one great concrete grid.

These events alarmed urban progressives such as James R. Ellis who could see the sprawl and environmental damage to come. Their solution was a new form of "home rule" government for King County with the power to regulate growth and provide essential services such as mass transit. The proposed charter was denounced as "communistic" by critics, especially on the Eastside, and failed in 1952. The following year, Bellevue incorporated as a city, and its leading developer, Kemper Freeman, began expanding Bellevue Square on former strawberry fields.

Farming was still the main business in south King County, but annual floods on the White and Green rivers frequently wiped out crops and drowned whole communities. Mud Mountain Dam provided partial relief in 1948 and State Legislator Howard Hanson campaigned relentlessly for additional flood control measures to protect the area's farmlands. Work began on his namesake dam in 1959, but by holding the rivers in check, it also unleashed the commercial and industrial development that would ultimately pave over the valley with factories, shopping centers, and parking lots.

Meanwhile, Jim Ellis and his allies in groups such as the Municipal League reorganized and returned to the polls in 1958 with a plan for a "Municipality of Metropolitan Seattle" to do regional planning, establish parks, and run key transit and waste disposal services. After their first plan was defeated in the spring, they succeeded in selling a scaled down Metro proposal to clean up Lake Washington — which suburban sewage had transformed into a veritable cesspool.

Creation of Metro was the first tentative step toward regional growth management, but some feared that it was already too late. While writing *Travels with Charley*, John Steinbeck visited Seattle in 1960 for the first time in several decades. He was appalled by what he saw —

> *On the outskirts of this place I once knew well I could not find my way. Along what had been country lanes rich with berries, high wire fences and mile-long factories stretched, and the yellow smoke of progress hung over all, fighting the sea winds' efforts to drive them off.*

Dorothy Bullitt

71

Filipino author Carlos Bulosan dies in Seattle on September 11, 1956.

Elvis shakes up Seattle on September 1. 1957.

Immense fire destroys Ballard cedar mill on May 20, 1958.

King County voters approve revised Municipality of Metropolitan Seattle (Metro) plan on September 9, 1958.

UW scientist collects a blood sample in the Congo in 1959 which turns out to contain the first documented AIDS virus.

Groundbreaking ceremonies for Howard A. Hanson Dam are held on February 3, 1959.

Seattle Public Library's new central library building is dedicated in 1960.

UW physicians led by Dr. Belding Scribner invent practical kidney dialysis system in 1960.

Port of Seattle expansion is approved by King County voters on November 8, 1960.

Population of Seattle tops 550,000 and that of King County tops 925,000 in 1960.

Metro rallied support with this photo of kids on the shore of polluted Lake Washington

1961~1970: Changing Times

Historians are still debating when the dramatic social changes that define the 1960s really began. Was the spark struck by John Kennedy's election, the first modern civil rights protests, the Vietnam War, the debut of the Beatles... or by some other seminal event?

In the case of Seattle, at least, the answer is clear: the Sixties began here on April 21, 1962, with the opening of the Century 21 Exposition. Planning for Seattle's second World's Fair began in 1957, chiefly at the behest of City Councilman Al Rochester, who had attended the Alaska-Yukon-Pacific Exposition in 1909 and thought Seattle should do it again on that fair's 50th anniversary. It took a little longer for organizers such as Joe Gandy and Eddie Carlson to pull it off, but they beat out New York City for the official blessing as the decade's first certified World's Fair.

Beyond giving the community a new totem in the Space Needle, a taste of modern transit with the Monorail, and a new civic commons at Seattle Center, this remarkable event opened Seattle's windows to the world and helped to air out the town's stuffy atmosphere of provincialism, prejudice, and prudishness — with a little kick from "Gay Way" producer Gracie Hansen. The fair created new venues and audiences for the arts that would revive the Seattle Symphony and seed the Seattle Repertory Theater, Seattle Opera,

Timeline

Coach Jim Owens leads UW Huskies to second consecutive Rose Bowl championship on January 2, 1961.

Boeing launches first Minuteman Intercontinental Ballistic Missile (ICBM) from Cape Canaveral on February 1, 1961.

Rev. Dr. Martin Luther King Jr. and President John F. Kennedy pay separate visits to Seattle during November 1961.

Seattle elects Wing Luke to the City Council on March 17, 1962.

Century 21 World's Fair opens on April 21, 1962.

Teamster President Dave Beck goes to prison for tax fraud on June 20, 1962.

Port of Seattle dedicates new Shilshole Marina on December 15, 1962.

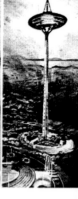

From Doodle to Needle

The concept for the Space Needle was born in 1959 when Seattle World's Fair Commission chair Edward E. "Eddie" Carlson dined in a restaurant atop Stuttgart, Germany's broadcast tower. Convinced that the World's Fair needed a similar "restaurant in the sky" as an attraction and symbol, Carlson sketched his idea on postcards to Fair officials. Architects John Graham Jr., Victor Steinbrueck, and John Ridley went to work turning Carlson's doodle into reality. When King County declined to fund the project, five private investors, Bagley Wright, Ned Skinner, Norton Clapp, John Graham Jr., and Howard S. Wright, took over and built the 605-foot tower in less than a year. The Needle opened shortly before the Century 21 Exposition on March 24, 1962. Thirty-seven years later, Seattle's monument to the future was designated an official landmark of the past.

Early ideas for the Space Needle and Ford's six-wheeled "Seattleite" concept car

Welcomes Cool and Warm

The Rev. Dr. Martin Luther King Jr. (lower right) paid his only visit to Seattle in November 1961, at the invitation of the Rev. Samuel B. McKinney (lower left), Mount Zion Baptist Church pastor and a friend and classmate of King at Atlanta's Morehouse College. McKinney arranged for Dr. King to speak at First Presbyterian Church because Mount Zion would not be large enough, but the church reneged and sponsors scrambled to find other venues. The following week, President John F. Kennedy received a much warmer welcome as he saluted the University of Washington's first century and Senator Warren Magnuson's first quarter century in Congress.

Wing Luke

First Boeing 727 trijet takes off from Renton Airport on February 9, 1963.

On February 14, 1963, Central Association proposes demolition of Pike Place Market.

Washington State forms Commission on the Status of Women on February 20, 1963.

Metro diverts first treated waste from Lake Washington on February 23, 1963.

PONCHO holds its first arts auction on April 27. 1963.

Seattle climber Jim Whittaker reaches Mount Everest summit on May 1, 1963.

Seattle City Council authorizes a Human Rights Commission on July 1, 1963, after first local sit-in.

Poet Theodore Roethke dies on August 1, 1963.

Seattle authorizes its first Urban Renewal project on August 23, 1963.

Evergreen Point Floating Bridge opens on August 28. 1963.

and Pacific Northwest Ballet, and the PONCHO philanthropy, among other groups. It also turned a profit while serving nearly 10 million visitors over its five-month run.

Cold War Fever

President John F. Kennedy, who had visited Seattle in November 1961 to help mark the centennial of the University of Washington, was scheduled to preside over the World's Fair conclusion on October 21, 1962. He cancelled at the last moment, pleading that he had a cold. Actually, he was grappling with the discovery that the Soviet Union had begun basing nuclear missiles in Cuba, a ploy which almost turned the Cold War red hot.

Boeing was by then providing much of America's strategic arsenal thanks to contracts for the B-52 bomber and Minuteman ICBM. It was also tapped early in the Apollo program to build the powerful Saturn V booster that would send humans to the moon by the decade's end. The debut of the 727 trijet in 1963 kept the Renton assembly line busy for a decade, but airlines proved initially cool toward the later 737 "Baby Boeing," which would ultimately become the company's biggest seller.

Following Kennedy's assassination in November 1963, however, the Pentagon would turn a cold shoulder. Boeing was stunned by the immediate cancellation of its contract for the X-20 "Dyna-Soar" space plane (which would have beat the Space Shuttle to orbit by nearly 20 years) and rejection of its bid for the giant C-5 military transport. Boeing made lemonade out of the latter reversal by recycling some of its design work to create the 747 Jumbo Jet, which debuted five years later.

Keepers of the Dream

The necessity of entertaining tens of thousands of international visitors during the World's Fair helped to undermine Seattle's restrictive "blue laws" and to energize its civil rights movement. A month before the Fair opened, Seattle voters elected the City Council's

First launch of a Minuteman ICBM, 1961 (Boeing Company)

first member of color, Chinatown leader Wing Luke, who also became the continental United States' highest Chinese American public official at the time.

Luke was a leader for numerous causes including historic preservation, neighborhood programs, and, above all, open housing reforms. A reluctant City Council finally put a ban on racial discrimination in rentals and home ownership to a public vote in March 1964, and it was rejected by two to one. Ironically, the King County Commissioners had enacted open housing just a week earlier without controversy.

Theodore Roethke (Mary Randlett)

Luke died in a 1965 plane crash with civil rights leader Sidney Gerber before he could resume the fight.

Other leaders filled the gap, ranging from Mt. Zion Baptist Church pastor Samuel McKinney, who hosted the Rev. Martin Luther King Jr's only Seattle visit in 1961, to more militant activists such as black contractors Tyree Scott and Eddie Rye, Black Panthers Elmer and Aaron Dixon, and Black Students Union leaders Larry Gossett and E.J. Brisker. Each made an impact and helped to break down the overt and covert barriers to racial equality in Seattle.

The University of Washington, a new community college system, and the Seattle School District became major battlefields in a campaign for integration that still continues. The cause of civil rights and social reform would broaden by the end of the 1960s to include Chicanos and other racial minorities, women, sexual minorities, and the disabled.

Urban Visions and Divisions

The World's Fair offered a glimpse of an idealized metropolis, complete with interurban monorails, domed stadiums, and abundant nuclear energy. Metro tried

President John F. Kennedy is assassinated on November 22, 1963.

Local tribes and supporters stage first "fish-in" to protest denial of treaty rights on March 2, 1964.

Seattle voters reject Open Housing Referendum on March 10, 1964.

Seattle Opera debuts with *Tosca* on May 7, 1964.

Gulf of Tonkin Resolution marks active involvement of the U.S. in the Vietnam War on August 7, 1964.

Beatles play at the Seattle Center Coliseum on August 21, 1964.

Monorail on 5th Avenue, ca. 1963

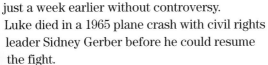

Preservation architects Ralph Anderson (left), Al Bumgardner, Ibsen Nelsen, Fred Bassetti, and Victor Steinbrueck in1984 (Mary Randlett)

Senator Dan Evans bucks the Lyndon Johnson landslide to defeat incumbent Governor Al Rosellini on November 7, 1964.

Major earthquake rattles Seattle on April 29, 1965.

Captive killer whale Namu arrives in Seattle on July 27, 1965.

Some 350 march downtown in Seattle's first demonstration against the Vietnam war on October 16, 1965.

Bellevue Community College opens on January 3, 1966.

Seattle population peaks at 574,000 in 1965 according to state estimates.

to tap this optimism in 1962 by asking King County voters for authority to plan a regional transit system, but voters declined to climb aboard.

By then, construction of Interstate 5 was well advanced, and city planners proposed a parallel expressway through eastern and central Seattle, which they named for legendary city engineer R.H. Thomson. Suburban leaders clamored for new highways such as the Evergreen Point Floating Bridge and an expanded Interstate 90 across Lake Washington to fuel growth in their communities. At one point, five floating bridges were on the state's drawing boards.

In a famous 1965 speech, regionalist Jim Ellis denounced this sprawling web of concrete and development as "a cause for rebellion." To contain and direct growth, he proposed a package of "Forward Thrust" public investments, including mass transit, new parks, low income housing, and a domed sports stadium. Most passed in 1968 — but not the rail system that would weave the parts together. A second try also failed in 1970, but at least King County began modernizing its government in 1969 under a new Home Rule charter.

Ambitious plans were also hatched within Seattle. The powerful Central Association (now the Downtown Seattle Association) proposed to flatten Pike Place Market and Pioneer Square for new apartments, offices, and parking garages linked by a system of ring roads. These urban renewal and highway schemes horrified visionary architects

Life, death, resurrection, and replacement of Pioneer Square's Occidental and Seattle Hotels, 1880-1963

including Victor Steinbrueck, Ibsen Nelsen, Fred Bassetti, Ralph Anderson, and Al Bumgardner, who helped to revive an urban design coalition through Allied Arts of Seattle.

They were joined by highway opponents such as the Central Seattle Community Council Federation and liberal attorneys and professionals in CHECC (Choose an Effective City Council). The latter scored its first victories in 1967 with the election of Phyllis Lamphere and Tim Hill, while Sam Smith became the first black to serve on the Council. More reformers would follow in subsequent elections, while Democratic State Senator Wes Uhlman won the 1969 race for mayor in a dramatic leftward shift of political power away from the business establishment. By then, however, this was not enough for the growing ranks of young activists mobilized by their opposition to the war in Vietnam.

A Whale's Song

The world's first captive killer whale, Namu, arrived for display at the private Seattle Marine Aquarium on Pier 56 on July 27, 1965. The 12-ton orca had become entangled in fishing nets in Namu Bay, British Columbia, and was later purchased by aquarium owner Ted Griffin and towed to Seattle in a floating pen. Namu died after a year, prompting calls for protection of marine mammals.

77

FRINGIE

Power to the People

The War in Vietnam and its domestic opposition so dominate today's perception of the 1960s that we forget that both developed relatively late in the decade. Seattle's first demonstration against the war drew fewer than 400 on a drizzly Saturday in October 1965, and the local chapter of Students for a Democratic Society (SDS) barely had enough members to fill a VW Microbus.

The related and simultaneous emergence of a local "counter-culture" also started small and slow on the fringe of the University of Washington. Indeed, before the term "hippie" arrived from California, University Way merchants labeled the Ave's growing throng of long-haired, guitar-strumming, and pot-smoking youth "fringies."

They listened to "alternative radio"

Seattle leaders unveil plan to demolish most of Pioneer Square on August 10, 1966.

Interstate 5 completed from Everett to Tacoma on January 31, 1967.

Helix, Seattle's first underground newspaper, debuts on March 23, 1967.

Ferry *Kalakala* ends service on Puget Sound on August 6, 1967.

Seattle voters elect "CHECC" reformers and first African American, Sam Smith, to the City Council on November 7, 1967.

Forward Thrust vote approves Kingdome and rejects light rail transit, on February 13, 1968.

Bobo the gorilla dies at Woodland Park Zoo on February 22, 1968.

Central Area riots follow assassination of Rev. Dr. Martin Luther King Jr. on April 5, 1968.

Immigration and Naturalization Act raises Asian American quotas on July 1, 1968.

Sky River Rock — And Mud

Inspired by the huge crowd that turned out in April 1968 to watch a piano drop from a helicopter at Larry Van Over's Duvall farm, counter-culture impresarios Paul Dorpat, John Chambless, and Cyrus Noe began planning the nation's first multi-day outdoor rock festival. They found a natural amphitheater on Betty Nelson's organic berry farm near Sultan, on the Skykomish River, and dubbed the event the Sky River Rock Festival and Lighter than Air Fair. Scores of bands agreed to perform, and the Grateful Dead paid a surprise visit on the event's last day. It rained most of that 1968 Labor Day weekend, and most patrons neglected to pay admission, but no one seemed to mind. Additional Sky River Rock Festivals were staged in Tenino in 1969 and near Vancouver, Washington, in 1970.

Southcenter Mall opens in Tukwila on July 31, 1968.

Sky River Rock Festival and Lighter Than Air Fair opens a three-day run near Sultan on August 30, 1968.

Rainiers play last Pacific Coast League game in Sicks' Stadium on September 2, 1968.

on KRAB-FM and clustered in and around coffee houses, psychedelic boutiques, and radical bookstores. They pursued "higher education" at the Free University and read an underground newspaper called the *Helix*. Thousands trekked to Duvall to watch (and hear) a piano drop from a helicopter and thousands more later frolicked in the mud at the Sky River Rock Festival in Sultan — while Soviet troops crushed the Prague Spring and Chicago police clubbed "Yippies" at the 1968 Democratic National Convention.

Thanks to mounting casualties in Vietnam — and mounting tensions at home — protests against U.S. policies and mainstream American culture became increasingly more militant, and the reaction of police and authorities escalated in kind. The Central Area was rocked by riots after Rev. Dr. Martin Luther King Jr.'s assassination in 1968, and the U District was

Kiss the Sky

Today, Seattle proudly boasts of being the hometown of Jimi Hendrix, and it celebrates his influences with Paul Allen's lavish Experience Music Project, but the artist's local ties were much more tangled. Born here in 1942, he taught himself to play a ukelele before graduating to an electric guitar. He played local gigs and got in trouble with the law as a teen, and then hit the road backing stars such as Little Richard. Hendrix's talents were finally recognized in England, and he returned stateside for a triumphant performance at the 1967 Monterey Pops Festival. His hometown reception was much cooler at his first local concert a year later, and Hendrix supposedly declared, "I hate Seattle." Drugs and the rock-n-roll lifestyle caught up with him in London, where he died in 1970. He came home permanently that year and now resides in a Renton cemetery.

Edwin Pratt

Here Come The Brides, based on the Mercer Girls, debuts on ABC on September 25, 1968.

Boeing rolls out first 747 Jumbo Jet in Everett on September 30, 1968.

King County voters approve first Home Rule Charter on November 5, 1968.

Civil Rights leader Edwin Pratt is murdered outside of his Shoreline home on January 26, 1969.

Consortium of oil companies announces plan for trans-Alaska pipeline on February 11, 1969.

John Spellman becomes first King County Executive on March 11, 1969.

SeaFirst Bank dedicates its new 50-story headquarters at 1001 4th Avenue on March 28, 1969.

Pilots play and win their first Major League baseball game on April 8, 1969.

Thousands protest planned R.H. Thomson Expressway through Arboretum on May 4, 1969.

LIBERATING THE FREEWAY

On May 5, 1970, an estimated 1,500 people surged onto southbound lanes of the Interstate 5 Freeway from NE 45th Street to protest the recent invasion of Cambodia and the deaths of four antiwar demonstrators on the Kent State campus in Ohio the previous day. The protesters halted all traffic as they moved south over the Freeway Bridge. They were met on the far side by a handful of State Troopers and exited peacefully at the Roanoke Street off-ramp. More than 10,000 tried to duplicate the "Freeway March" on the following day, but were repulsed by State Troopers and police with tear gas and clubs. On May 8, Mayor Wes Uhlman closed the I-5 Express Lanes for a sanctioned anti-war march from downtown Seattle to the University District by some 15,000 demonstrators. Above: Protesters occupy I-5 at NE 45th Street (Alan Lande)

SONIC BUST

On December 3, 1970, the U.S. Senate rejected a last-gasp proposal to continue development of the Boeing prototype of a civil supersonic transport, or SST, which had begun with great hope in 1966. The project encountered engineering and budgetary problems, and environmental studies suggested that large fleets of SSTs could damage the upper atmosphere. The Senate's rejection of new funding killed the project and precipitated the immediate layoff of 7,500 Boeing workers. Meanwhile, the Soviet Union flew the TU-144 while Great Britain and France developed the Concorde. In a final indignity, Boeing auctioned its full-scale SST mockup to a Florida amusement park.

Dorian House offers Seattle's first Gay counseling service on July 7, 1969.

Apollo 11 lands on the moon on July 20, 1969.

Young people battle police at Alki Beach and in the University District between August 10 and 15, 1969.

UW enrollment tops 32,600 in September 1969.

Seattle Police Chief Frank Ramon resigns amid gambling payoff scandal on October 8, 1969.

Wes Uhlman is elected Seattle mayor on November 4, 1969.

Uwajimaya's, Seattle's largest Asian retail store, opens in 1970.

Seattle Liberation Front clashes with police at the Federal Courthouse on February 17, 1970, leading to trial of the "Seattle Seven."

Medic One emergency cardiac service becomes operational on March 7, 1970.

shut down for nearly a week in 1969 by running battles between police, teenagers, and "street people." In February 1970, protesters led by the new Seattle Liberation Front clashed with police at the Federal Courthouse, and SLF leaders were later tried as the "Seattle Seven."

The most dramatic confrontations followed the U.S. invasion of Cambodia and subsequent deaths of antiwar protesters on Ohio's Kent State campus. On May 5, 1970, more than 1,500 demonstrators briefly and peacefully "occupied" Interstate 5 in the U District and shut down the UW campus. Protests turned violent the next day and night, and vigilante off-duty policemen prowled the U District randomly beating anyone they could find.

Seattle achieved the dubious distinction of suffering the most bombings and arson fires per capita of any American city. Meanwhile, respect for the police crumbled amid revelations of wide-scale gambling payoffs. While the Vietnam War still dominated headlines in 1970, local activists found new and ultimately more enduring causes: neighborhood empowerment, environmental protection, and equal rights for women and sexual minorities which would set the agenda for the coming decade.

Both sides of the cultural and generational divide eventually exhausted themselves and the violence subsided in the new decade. The community also found something more immediate and personal to worry about as tens of thousands of workers lost their jobs amid a deepening national aerospace recession known locally as the "Boeing Bust."

Bobo as a pet, early 1950s

Best Laid Plans

During the 1950s, state and city planners drew up plans for an elaborate network of huge multi-lane highways and bridges for the Puget Sound region, but by the time they were ready to start moving dirt around in the 1960s, the political landscape had shifted dramatically. Regional visionaries advocated light rail as the better vehicle for transporting commuters, conservationists feared the loss of wilderness and open space, and urban neighborhoods lined the ramparts to block the bulldozers headed their way. Anti-highway forces found a powerful new legal weapon in the Environmental Impact Statement (EIS), an otherwise innocuous analytical exercise mandated by new federal environmental laws. Through legal challenge of the "adequacy" of an EIS, opponents of unwanted roads and development could stall public projects for years. As a result, initial plans (pictured right) for Interstate 90 were dramatically scaled back, and proposals such as Seattle's R.H. Thomson Expressway and Bay Freeway were abandoned or vetoed. Unfortunately, voters simultaneously rejected Metro and Forward Thrust plans for rail transit, laying the foundation for today's gridlock.

Political Scientist?

Dixy Lee Ray reigns as one of the most distinctive public personalities to emerge in Seattle during the 1960s. A UW professor of marine biology, she took over the new Pacific Science Center in 1963 and established the former World's Fair pavilion as a popular museum and education resource. She also battled city hall in a long, unsuccessful campaign to build a public research aquarium at Golden Gardens near Ballard. President Nixon appointed her to the Atomic Energy Commission in 1972, where she boosted nuclear power plants and bashed environmentalists. Despite her anti-Green rhetoric, Washington voters made her governor four years later, then reconsidered after one stormy term. She retired to her Fox Island compound in southern Puget Sound and raised pigs named after her least favorite reporters until her death in 1994.

Bob Satiacum, Bernie Whitebear, Jane Fonda, and others attempt to occupy Fort Lawton on March 8, 1970.

Seattle observes first Earth Day on April 22, 1970.

Anti-war demonstrators briefly occupy Interstate 5 on May 5, 1970.

All four Forward Thrust bonds fail on May 19, 1970.

Opponents of expanded Interstate 90 file first environmental lawsuit on May 28, 1970.

Washington voters legalize abortion on November 3, 1970.

Boeing begins massive layoffs after the Supersonic Transport (SST) loses funding on December 3, 1970.

Population of Seattle shrinks to 530,000, less than half of total King County population of 1,150,000, in 1970.

1971~2000:
A Global Village

Caught in the downdraft of the airlines industry and national economy, Boeing jettisoned more than 60,000 jobs between 1961 and 1971. The rest of the Puget Sound economy plummeted with its leading employer, and a pair of young real estate agents named Jim Youngren and Bob McDonald decided to pierce the gloom with a little humor. They leased a billboard near Sea-Tac with the message, "Will the last person leaving Seattle -- Turn out the lights." Nobody laughed.

An early casualty of the Boeing Bust was the latest attempt to

FESTIVAL '72
SEATTLE CENTER
JULY 21-22-23

fund light rail transit, which failed with the second round of Forward Thrust bonds in 1970. The region's existing bus system was in free fall, and County Executive John Spellman, Seattle Mayor Wes Uhlman, and Metro guru Jim Ellis joined forces to return to the voters one last time with a plan for a "rubber-tire" transit system based on buses, electric trolleys, and an expanded network of park and ride lots.

On September 19, 1972, taxpayers finally climbed aboard. The following year, Uhlman's staff suggested that riders should be able to ride without charge within downtown Seattle. Metro Transit tried it, and with a few new restrictions, downtown bus travel remains free to this day.

New Federalism

President Richard Nixon responded to the Boeing Bust with emergency employment funds, special grants, and the nation's first (and last) experiment with a guaranteed annual income as a substitute for traditional welfare. Of course, it didn't hurt that Washington's two U.S. Senators, Warren G. Magnuson and Henry "Scoop" Jackson, were among the most powerful men in Congress.

Under the rubric of a "New Federalism" Nixon and, after his resignation, Gerald Ford promoted revenue sharing and block grants as alternatives to traditional grants such as Model Cities and Urban Renewal. The latter had been a dismal failure in Seattle and the prod for successful campaigns to save Pike Place Market and Pioneer Square from federally-funded bulldozers. Most federal urban aid was consolidated into annual Community Development Block Grants in 1974. Although the sums flowing to Seattle shrank, the city gained greater freedom to plan and run programs in partnership with citizens and community groups.

The New Federalism also embodied a "new regionalism" which gave suburbs a stronger hand in regional planning bodies such as today's Puget Sound Regional Council. This reflected a general population shift in which Seattle actually shrank from 574,000 in the mid-1960s to 493,000 in 1980, while the rest of the county ballooned to 750,000. It also set the stage for provincial battles over transportation and growth management between generally conservative suburban officials and their more liberal urban counterparts.

From Protest to Process

The United States' slow, painful withdrawal from Vietnam blunted the war as a domestic issue but it did not stifle social and political activism on other fronts. Long suppressed grievances bubbled to the surface as women, gays, lesbians, Native Americans, and racial minorities demanded their rights and fair slices of the American pie. Seattle's African Americans also won their long campaign to desegregate the city's schools, but mandatory busing would create as many problems as it solved. The war's end also brought new challenges for the assimilation of tens of thousands of Southeast Asian refugees, for the reintegration of

Washington state passes Equal Rights Amendment to state constitution on November 29, 1972.

Metro Transit establishes free downtown bus zone in September 1973.

Gas Works Park opens in Seattle's Wallingford neighborhood in 1974.

Federal Judge George Boldt affirms Native American treaty fishing rights on February 12, 1974.

Seattle's first Gay Pride Week begins on June 24, 1974.

Vietnam War ends with fall of Saigon on April 30, 1975.

Seattle dedicates Sand Point Park (later Magnuson Park) on December 26, 1975.

Kingdome opens to a crowd of 54,000 on March 27, 1976.

Seattle Seahawks play their first game on September 12, 1976.

GOING TO MARKET

On November 2, 1971, Seattle voters approved Initiative No.1 to "preserve, improve and restore the Pike Place Market" and "prohibit alterations, demolition, or construction" without approval of a new 12 member commission. The election marked the culmination of a campaign begun in 1964 and led chiefly by architect Victor Steinbrueck. Credit is also due government leaders and project managers who then found and managed the tens of millions of dollars needed to restore the Market's decaying warren of shops and stalls.

Indian leader Bernie Whitebear

Pioneer Square's first Fat Tuesday celebration begins on February 14, 1977.

Mariners play their first baseball game in Seattle on April 6, 1977.

Seattle Aquarium opens on May 20, 1977.

Seattle voters elect Charles Royer as mayor on November 8, 1977.

Freighter *Chavez* rams West Seattle Bridge on June 11, 1978.

Seattle Schools begin mandatory busing on September 29, 1978.

Seattle voters uphold gay and lesbian rights by rejecting Initiative 13 on November 7, 1978.

Microsoft Corporation opens first Eastside office in December 1978.

China-U.S. trade resumes as M.V. *Liulinhai* docks at Port of Seattle on April 18, 1979.

veterans, and for coping with the 1960s hangover of drug abuse and inner city stagnation.

The confrontational tactics of the Vietnam opposition were applied to local issues as Chicanos occupied an abandoned Beacon Hill school to create El Centro de la Raza, and Indians (with Jane Fonda) stormed Fort Lawton and won development of Daybreak Star Center as part of a new Discovery Park. The courts were also busy in the early 1970s: federally mandated redistricting adjusted the state's political representation to reflect its true population, Judge George Boldt affirmed Indian treaty rights to half of the region's salmon harvest, and the new National Enviromental Policy Act (sponsored in 1970 by U.S. Senator Henry Jackson) was turned

into a powerful legal weapon by opponents of new highways such as I-90 and other unwanted development.

Under Mayor Wes Uhlman and his three-term successor, former KING-TV commentator Charles Royer, Seattle institutionalized new mechanisms to accommodate cultural diversity and citizen participation without paralyzing government. While some joked that "process is our most important product," Seattle actually made remarkable progress in the face of economic and political adversity during the 1970s and 1980s, evidenced by a legacy of new parks such as Gas Works, Discovery, Sand Point-Magnuson, the Seattle Aquarium, and an improved Woodland Park Zoo.

Along the way, Seattle won universal praise as

HistoryLink animation of Kingdome's construction

"America's most livable city." It could also finally lay claim to playing in the "big leagues," as the Kingdome opened in 1976 to host the Seahawks and the Mariners, and the Super-Sonics brought home the NBA crown in 1979.

Action and Reaction

The eruption of Mount St. Helens on May 18, 1980, spared Seattle, but the "Reagan Land-slide" that November would rattle the city's political foundations. After half a century of generally liberal federal policy, Seattle found itself increasingly out of step with the conservative administration. It also lost Congressional seniority with Slade Gorton's defeat of Warren G. Magnuson in 1980 and Henry Jackson's death three years later. Neither Gorton's skills nor the election of former three-term governor Dan Evans to finish Jackson's term could restore the region's former political clout.

At the same time, King County suburbs bustled with new development and confidence. Kemper Freeman Jr. and other investors transformed Bellevue from a sleepy bedroom community into an "edge city" complete with its own skyscrapers. Research and office parks spread across the Eastside to house new companies such as Microsoft, founded in 1975 by Lakeside School chums Paul Allen and Bill Gates. King County's population outside Seattle would grow to nearly a million by 1990.

"Industrial sculpture" at Gas Works Park

SuperSonics win NBA Championship on June 1, 1979.

Mount St. Helens erupts on May 18, 1980.

King County Executive John Spellman is elected governor on November 4, 1980

Population of Seattle drops below 500,000 while all of King County grows to 1,250,000 in 1980.

Sheihk Idriss Mosque, Seattle's first Islamic temple, opens in 1981.

Filipino labor activists Gene Viernes and Silme Domingo are slain in Seattle on June 1, 1981.

Seattle Waterfront Streetcar inaugurates service on May 29, 1982.

Green River killer's first victim, Wendy Lee Coffield, is found on July 15, 1982.

Three robbers kill 13 patrons of Wah Mee gambling club on February 18, 1983.

The Seattle Times and the *Seattle Post-Intelligencer* enter Joint Operating Agreement on May 23, 1983.

BENSON'S FOLLY

Many scoffed at City Council Member George Benson when he proposed establishment of a streetcar along the downtown waterfront. The line was an instant success when it opened in 1982 and was later extended through Pioneer Square to the International District. Benson was also a leader in saving the Monorail during construction of Westlake Center and in laying tracks in the downtown transit tunnel for future light rail.

REDOING THE ZOO

On November 5, 1985, King County voters approved $31.5 million in bonds for Seattle's Woodland Park Zoo. The bonds financed award-winning bioclimatic exhibits and a new elephant house (shown before and after), making Woodland Park one of the world's most ecologically sensitive zoos.

Columbia Center, tallest building in Seattle, opens on March 2, 1985.

County voters approve Woodland Park Zoo bonds on November 5, 1985.

Uncompleted Husky Stadium spectator stands collapse on February 25, 1987.

Cal Anderson becomes Washington's first openly gay state legislator in 1987.

Boeing wins prime contract for International Space Station on December 1, 1987.

Washington State Convention and Trade Center officially opens on June 23, 1988.

Mayor Royer promoted denser zoning to expand the city's housing supply, and economic recovery spurred construction of new downtown skyscrapers. Martin Selig launched a one-man building boom in the Denny Regrade and then topped himself — and everyone else — with the 76-story Columbia Center, which became the West's tallest office building in 1985.

Meanwhile, Metro descended below downtown's streets to dig a transit tunnel from the new Convention and Trade Center to the International District. The retail core was further clogged by construction of the Westlake Center and adjacent park, which had been the object of decades of debate. All this dust proved too much for a majority of Seattle voters who voted in May 1989 to "cap" downtown building heights. Preservationists also fought successfully to save landmarks such as the Blue Moon Tavern and unsuccessfully for the Music Hall Theater, although its demise prompted new laws to protect the Paramount, Moore, and other historic downtown theaters.

Mayor Norm Rice

In 1989, Seattle City Attorney Doug Jewett sponsored an initiative to end city support for mandatory busing and campaigned for mayor. Norman Rice, only the second African American to sit on the City Council, emerged from a crowded primary field to challenge Jewett. Rice won a decisive victory in the November election, while Jewett's initiative squeaked through. It soon became academic as the school district shifted gears on busing.

John Stamets caught the collapse of Husky Stadium's bleachers on February 25, 1987

Metro drew fire from critics who viewed its federated council of elected officials as aloof and unaccountable in guiding expensive and controversial projects such as the new West Point sewage treatment plant and downtown bus tunnel. Federal judge William Dwyer agreed on September 6, 1990, and ruled Metro's governance structure unconstitutional — just as the first buses rolled through the downtown tunnel.

University Station of Metro's downtown transit tunnel

As if presaging the next decade's struggles over regional transportation and growth, the original Lake Washington Floating Bridge sank in a storm on Thanksgiving Day 1990.

Foreign Affairs

As the Soviet Union crumbled, Communist China opened its economy, and an international alliance ejected Iraqi occupiers from Kuwait, President George H.W. Bush proclaimed the dawn of a "new world order." That it was a new world, there was no doubt, but it would turn out to be anything but orderly.

At the outset of the 1990s, King County was bullish on the prospects for international trade and commerce. Thanks to Boeing, Microsoft, Starbucks, Amazon.com, Immunex, cell phone pioneers Craig and Bruce McCaw, and a host of other enterprises and entrepreneurs — not to mention grunge rock stars such as Kurt Cobain — the region was a recognized world leader in technology, e-commerce, and consumer culture. Seattle's prominence in the global economy was saluted by its selection to host the Asia Pacific Economic Cooperation conference in 1993. The event, which was attended by President Bill Clinton and Pacific Rim leaders, went so smoothly that Seattle soon pursued the opportunity to host the next major round of World Trade Organization negotiations in 2000.

Florida executes serial killer and former Seattleite Ted Bundy on January 24, 1989.

Voters "CAP" downtown building heights on May 16, 1989.

Norm Rice wins election as Seattle's first African American mayor on November 7, 1989.

Ted Turner's Goodwill Games open in Seattle on July 20, 1990.

Federal District Judge William Dwyer rules Metro Council unconstitutional on September 6, 1990.

Bus service begins in downtown Seattle transit tunnel on September 15, 1990.

Original Lake Washington Floating Bridge sinks on November 25, 1990.

Dr. E. Donnall Thomas shares 1990 Nobel Prize for medicine for bone marrow transplantation research at the Fred Hutchinson Cancer Research Center.

A WORK OF ART

During the installation of Jonathan Barofsky's "Hammering Man" at the new Downtown Seattle Art Museum on September 28, 1991, a strap supporting the 48-foot tall metal sculpture snapped and dropped the giant mechanical silhouette. Workers and spectators fled in terror while construction-documentarian John Stamets recorded the scene. The public art work was repaired and re-installed without incident as the new SAM opened in 1992.

Population of King County exceeds 1.5 million and Seattle rebounds to 515,000 in 1990 census.

First Seattle protest is held against the Gulf War on January 14, 1991.

Seattle Art Museum opens downtown on December 5, 1991.

Rioting erupts in Seattle following verdicts in Rodney King beating on May 1, 1992.

Frederick & Nelson department store goes out of business on May 31, 1992.

Voters amend King County Charter to assume Metro services on November 3, 1992, and elect former Congressman Mike Lowry governor.

Gary Locke becomes King County's first Chinese American Executive on November 2, 1993.

President Clinton convenes APEC summit on Blake Island on November 20, 1993.

Closer to Home

King County still faced major challenges at home in grappling with long-standing problems of transportation and suburban sprawl. The decade began with good news as the State Legislature mandated stronger growth management plans and controls and authorized the Puget Sound region to design and fund a multi-county rail and bus transit system.

A $3.9 billion plan for the latter passed on the second try in 1996, but early hopes were dashed as light rail costs soared and neighborhoods battled over routes. Cab driver-populist Dick Falkenbury and poet Grant Cogswell convinced gridlocked Seattle voters to approve an expanded and modernized Monorail system in 1997.

Under federal court order, King County government absorbed Metro's bus and water quality functions in 1992 and expanded its Council to 13 members to better represent the metropolitan area. At the same time, numerous communities incorporated as independent cities, reducing the County's direct service area and revenues.

When the venerable Frederick & Nelson department store folded in 1992, Mayor Norm Rice rallied both the business community and voters to re-open Pine Street to traffic (which Rice had closed two years before) through Westlake Park as a

Benaroya Hall

necessary condition for Nordstrom to take over the store. The city also helped to finance the Benaroya Hall for the Seattle Symphony, located next to the new downtown Seattle Art Museum, and the controversial Pacific Place shopping center and garage.

These actions succeeded in reviving downtown's sagging retail core, but they also antagonized neighborhood activists such as Charlie Chong who had already mobilized against Rice's vision of creating denser "urban villages" to help control suburban growth. A citizen proposal for a vast "Seattle Commons" park and related housing and commercial development south of Lake Union became a lightning rod in this debate and failed in 1995 and 1996 elections.

Fund and Games

Gary Locke became King County's first Chinese American Executive in 1993 and spent much his term grappling with threats by both the Mariners and Seahawks to bolt Seattle if something wasn't done about the aging Kingdome. Despite the Mariners' dramatic turnaround on the field, voters rejected bonds to build a new baseball stadium and upgrade the dome in 1995. Governor Mike Lowry (a former County Council Member and Congressman) and the Legislature interceded to pass a state funding package for today's Safeco Field.

Frank Gehry's EMP pavilion

Nirvana rock band star Kurt Cobain commits suicide on April 5, 1994.

Seattle School Board selects John Stanford as its first African American superintendent on September 1, 1995.

Voters reject Seattle Mariners stadium taxes on September 19, 1995.

Navy bids Sand Point naval base farewell on September 28, 1995.

Seattle Mariners win the American League West pennant on October 2, 1995.

Seattle voters twice reject proposed Seattle Commons Park near south Lake Union in 1995 and 1996.

Gary Locke becomes Governor and Sound Transit plan clears second vote on November 5, 1996; Ron Sims is appointed and later elected as the first African American King County Executive.

Seattle School Board votes to end mandatory busing for desegregation on November 20, 1996.

Washington voters fund new Seahawks stadium on June 17, 1997, and Paul Allen acquires the team.

Boeing merges with McDonnell Douglas on August 1, 1997.

Safeco Field at dusk (Seattle Mariners)

DOME'S DAY DONE

With Safeco Field finally built and funding for a new football stadium secured, judgment day arrived for the Kingdome on March 26, 2000. The world's largest self-supporting dome required eight years to design and build — and 16.8 seconds to collapse into a neat mountain of rubble.

Locke won election as governor in 1996, but the Kingdome crisis followed him to Olympia as Seahawks owner Ken Behring threatened to leave. Microsoft co-founder Paul Allen (Seattle Commons booster and father of the new Experience Music Project at Seattle Center) volunteered to take over the Seahawks if the public helped finance a substitute for the Kingdome. In June 1997, state voters narrowly passed a $300 million funding package for the new stadium, and Allen matched the taxpayers' commitment to fulfill his side of the bargain. On March 26, 2000, the Kingdome was imploded to make way for the Seahawks' new aerie.

New World Order?

After Mayor Rice declined to run for a third term, Seattle turned in 1997 to former developer and Port Commissioner Paul Schell (who had lost to Charles Royer 20 years earlier). He saw Seattle as a cosmopolitan hub in the emerging global economy, but his vision was not shared by all.

By 1999, labor, environmentalists, and human rights advocates in the United States and around the world were challenging "globalization." The World Trade Organization meetings had already drawn noisy protests in Europe, but Seattle hoped that its post-Sixties ethos of peaceful debate would cushion any dissent when the WTO convened here in late November 1999.

WTO battle lines at 4th and Pike, November 30, 1999

A Big Bundle of Joy

One bright spot at the 20th century's close was the birth of Hansa, a healthy 235-pound girl — elephant, that is — at the Zoo on November 3, 2000.

Rivers Run Through It

On March 16, 1999, nine salmon runs in the Pacific Northwest were listed by the Department of the Interior as endangered species, joining 15 other population groups of salmon already under federal protection. The listing covered most of Washington state and the entire Puget Sound basin — and was the first such designation to affect a metropolitan area. King County led formation of a regional task force to reduce industrial and agricultural pollution and to protect spawning habitats from development. Seattle Public Utilities restored urban streams and intensified its efforts in the Cedar River Watershed, and City Light expanded its award-winning habitat program on the upper Skagit River. Significantly, greater Seattle's water consumption has not grown since 1975 despite dramatic increases in population.

The gamble almost worked, but as some 50,000 WTO protesters marched peacefully, the world's TV cameras focused on a handful of self-styled anarchists who trashed downtown Nike stores, Starbucks, and other symbols of the global economy. Police reacted tardily and clumsily, leading to running battles with protesters in the downtown retail core, Denny Regrade, and Capitol Hill.

Mayor Schell reeled, Police Chief Norman Stamper resigned, and Seattle became synonymous with the anti-globalization movement. There was more bad news to come as Seattle prepared to celebrate the end of the Millennium (a year early, in the opinion of some). On December 14, 1999, an alert Port Angeles border guard detained an Algerian attempting to enter from Canada. His car contained the ingredients for a bomb, and he had a reservation for a motel room near Seattle Center, the focus of the city's Millennium bash.

Reluctantly and in the face of local criticism and national derision, Schell cancelled the New Century's Eve party. Later events would cast his decision in a new light.

Nine Puget Sound salmon runs are listed as Endangered Species on March 16, 1999.

Safeco Field opens on July 15, 1999.

Seattle protests against the World Trade Organization (WTO) begin on November 29, 1999.

Mayor Paul Schell cancels Seattle Center millennium eve celebration on December 31, 1999.

Bill & Melinda Gates Foundation becomes the nation's richest philanthropy on January 24, 2000.

Boeing engineers strike for 40 days beginning February 9, 2000.

Swedish Hospital merges with Providence Hospital on February 29, 2000.

Kingdome stadium is imploded on March 26, 2000.

Experience Music Project opens at Seattle Center on June 23, 2000.

Workers strike at *The Seattle Times* and the *Seattle Post-Intelligencer* on November 21, 2000.

Seattle population exceeds 563,000 and King County counts more than 1.7 million residents in 2000.

Future Shock

Pioneer Square's crippled Pergola

As rough as the last few years of the 20th century were for Seattle and King County, nothing prepared them for the first 10 months of the 21st. The year began with a bad omen when a wayward delivery truck clipped and toppled Pioneer Square's historic Pergola — an artifact of Seattle's first world's fair back in 1909.

Pioneer Square was the scene of a more disturbing social collapse during February's Fat Tuesday revelries. Drunken gangs of young men ran berserk through the streets, beating anyone who stood in their path. The police held back for fear of intensifying the violence while one group of thugs beat a man to death.

The day after Mardi Gras, the second worst earthquake in the region's recorded history rumbled across Puget Sound on Ash (or "Crash") Wednesday, damaging several buildings in Pioneer Square. The region's economic bedrock shuddered again less than a month later when Boeing president Phil Condit announced that the company would relocate its corporate headquarters out of its home city. Company executives ultimately roosted in a Chicago skyscraper.

Fairly or not, many blamed Mayor Paul Schell for the city's spate of Job-like tribulations. Schell had run a scandal-free administration and presided over the greatest public works program in the city's history with more than half a billion dollars committed to libraries, parks, community centers, Seattle Center improvements, and a new city hall and public safety complex — but he could not escape the shadow of WTO.

City Attorney Mark Sidran and Metropolitan King County Council Member Greg Nickels led a crowded field of challengers with starkly contrasting sets of civic values. Sidran, who earned both bouquets and brickbats for advocating "civility laws" to control panhandlers and the homeless, offered munici-

Rem Koolhaas concept for new downtown library. Upper right: Seahawks Stadium